"Mark Childress' puncture-sharp wit kept me sane during the Trumpian days of torment. What joy to have the complete compendium of horrors, delivered in the form of pure literary genius. The perfect alternative to Xanax or Zen meditation."
— *Amy Tan, author of THE JOY LUCK CLUB and*
WHERE THE PAST BEGINS

"You, sir, are a libtard."
— *Glenn Beck*

"I love every word Mark Childress writes, including this new compilation of his great political writing ... brilliant and hilarious."
— *Anne Lamott, author of BIRD BY BIRD and*
ALMOST EVERYTHING: NOTES ON HOPE

✧

"With covfefe strong, all the boats sailed along
Flying Trump flags from every railing
The waves rose up high but they zoomed right on by
All the libtards alongshore, a-wailing

And every man knew, as the captain did too,
Twas the witch of November come stealing!
Kamala's her name and they see her dark flame
Lighting up the skies o'er Sinky Trumpy

The boats were too close - two or three feet at most
And the big waves began now a buildin'-
The little boats sank, people fell in and drank
The dark waters of gloomy Lake Travis

When suppertime came the old man came on deck sayin'
Magas, it's too rough to feed ya
But at seven p.m. when the hatchway caved in, he said
Magas, it's been good to know ya!"

— *From "The Wreck of the S.S. Full MAGA"*

D0522467

THE
BOOK
OF
ORANGE

ALSO BY MARK CHILDRESS

Georgia Bottoms
One Mississippi
Gone for Good
Crazy in Alabama
Tender
V for Victor
A World Made of Fire

THE
BOOK
OF
ORANGE

A Journal of the Trump Years
By a Crazed Snowflake
Employing Rhyming Insults, Limericks,
Loathing, Hyperbole, Secret Transcripts,
Show Tunes, Mockery, Rants, Jokes, & Rude
Memes

MARK CHILDRESS

OVERTURE BOOKS ✧ NEW ORLEANS

Jacket design by Peter Thorpe
Photographs by the author
Produced for Overture Books by Quid Pro LLC, New Orleans

First Edition: November 2020
ISBN:9781610274272
www.markchildress.com

For Alan, Michele,
and my friends in the Resistance

THE
BOOK
OF
ORANGE

2015

Jul 30, 2015

Kids, don't you be laughing at Donald Trump. The last time the Republicans put forward a candidate this laughable, his name was Ronald Reagan and he served two terms.

Aug 22, 2015

Thirty thousand people did not come out to a stadium Friday night in Mobile, Alabama to hear Donald Trump talk about his kind and loving stance toward Mexicans. His racial arguments appeal to Alabama. He sings a song they've always loved to hear.

Donald Trump would be a disaster if Fate somehow allowed him to run this country for even one day. But he is doing a hell of a job running the news media at the moment.

Aug 26, 2015

Donald Trump told Jorge Ramos to "go back to Univision." It would be better for America if Donald Trump would go the hell back to Atlantic City and stay there.

Sep. 7, 2015

Cher said on Twitter that Donald Trump being in the lead in the GOP race is "like being the most athletic guy in the nursing home." Cher for President!

Sep 8, 2015

I dreamt last night of a Trump-Palin ticket – "You're fired! You betcha!"– then I woke up and thought, no, if there is a God, I am sure he thinks we are laughable but does he hate us that much?

Oct 29, 2015

Eight years ago they told us that unless we elected John McCain, the USA would collapse and we would all be lucky to eat one cans of beans a week. Four years ago they told us that unless we elected Mitt Romney, the USA would collapse and none of us would ever get an elevator for our cars. Last night they told us again and again that unless we elect one of them and NOT Hillary Clinton, the USA will collapse, millions of immigrants will swarm in and take all the jobs away that we lost because we elected Hillary Clinton.

Nov 23, 2015

Yes, Donald Trump could be elected President of the United States. A chimpanzee could, theoretically, write a novel. But it would not be a book you would want to curl up with.

Oct 2, 2015

For eight years the Republicans had to deal with the fact of a failing, inadequate Republican President who involved us in two unnecessary wars on false pretenses and, at the end, presided over the near-total wreck of the US economy.

In 2008, every Republican predicted doom for America if Obama was elected. Republicans in Congress did their best to sabotage Obama's every move, but he succeeded in spite of them.

After seven years of the Obama miracle – steadily improving economic conditions, despite the strenuous efforts of the Party of No to thwart him at every turn – Republicans simply can't admit they were wrong – that they have been wrong, continuously, for the past sixteen years.

So when someone like Trump brags about his success, when he tells them lie after lie, when he blares forth with racist bromides and insists he saw things that never happened – it just matches the GOP mood, which is all about the angry denial of reality.

Republicans love Trump for his lies, not in spite of them. He confirms the reality they want to believe. They were wrong, all of them – but he assures them they were right. And that's the only "news" they can bear to hear.

Dec 6, 2015

President Obama calls it "insanity" but I think he is just being polite. The same 45 Republican senators who call Obama "soft on terrorism" voted to allow people on the terror watch list to buy any kind of gun they'd like.

That's not just not bad judgment. To me it smells like treason: arming terrorists who actively seek to undermine the safety and security of the American people.

Dec 8, 2015

If I still have any Republican friends, I would love to hear someone denouncing the racist, fascist rhetoric emitted yesterday by the front-runner in your party's Presidential contest.

The deafening Republican silence is, if not agreement, at least complicity through failure to act. Every Republican must pledge not to support Trump as the GOP nominee.

Yes even you, Ted Cruz, we've noticed how very quiet you are about this.

 Donald J. Trump ✔
@realDonaldTrump   ○○○

I told you @TIME Magazine would never pick me as person of the year despite being the big favorite They picked person who is ruining Germany

7:53 AM · Dec 9, 2015 · Twitter for Android

6.5K Retweets   **1.1K** Quote Tweets   **8.7K** Likes

Dec 9, 2015

Trump's mad because TIME picked Angela Merkel as "Person of the Year." "The person who is ruining Germany," he complains.

Of course Donald has a few ideas for how *he* would straighten out Germany.

2016

Jan 3, 2016

"At a meeting with The Times's editorial writers, Mr. Trump talked about the art of applause lines. "You know," he said of his events, "if it gets a little boring, if I see people starting to sort of, maybe thinking about leaving, I can sort of tell the audience, I just say, 'We will build the wall!' and they go nuts."

Like that scene in "Blue Velvet" when Dennis Hopper snorted nitrous oxide through the face mask.

Jan 22, 2016

I heard that Sarah Palin can see Trump's next wife from her house.

Jan 23, 2016

Michael Bloomberg threatening to enter the race. Will he and Trump split the billionaire vote?

Jan 23, 2016

Trump said today he could "shoot somebody in the middle of Fifth Avenue" and not lose any votes. I suggest he try out his theory on himself first, just to make sure it works.

Feb 1, 2016

What is your least favorite expression of 2016? Mine is "and that's good news for Donald Trump."

Feb 22, 2016

Several of my friends are a little sad about the election. They pine for a third Obama term, or they want a Socialist Paradise on Earth Right Now, or they want Hillary to bring them a blankie and some nice hot cocoa. They aren't *excited* by our candidates. We don't have *fun demagogues* like Trump and Cruz. My friends want Hillary to have more charisma. They want Bernie to be more realistic.

I, on the other hand, feel a really weird excitement about it all – the thrill that comes from keeping a fucking maniac out of the White House.

Feb 24, 2016

"I love the poorly educated," says the victorious Trump.

Feb 29, 2016

I've got my bike and I've been trying to find a morning circuit that gets me out of Ha Noi's scooter exhaust and insane traffic. I ride across the Long Bien bridge, up the dyke of the Red River to No Bai bridge, then back through little villages to the ancient citadel town of Co Loa.

Mar 3, 2016

In 1860 did people on Facebook say "I never thought I'd say this, but that Jefferson Davis really speaks his mind?" Because I'm about to decide it's time for Mr. Lincoln to call for 100,000 volunteers.

Mar 4, 2016

Watching the "highlights" of the Republican debate, in which the leading Republican candidate for President assured voters about the size of his penis that "there's no problem." The crowd roared its delight.

Have we ever had a candidate for President who was this mentally ill? When was the last time millions of people were eager to be led by a megalomaniac narcissist with poor impulse control?

Mar 27, 2016

I never, ever, ever, *ever* thought I would hear the leading candidate for the Republican nomination casually call for torturing people. No code, no euphemisms. The Fox viewer is now so thoroughly misinformed that not a peep is heard from anyone on the right.

Mar 31, 2016

If the GOP nominates either Donald Trump or Ted Cruz, the GOP deserves to die.

In Ha Noi, the museum of the Vietnamese military speaks of the folly of an earlier generation of American leaders who thought it was their business to run the whole world.

Let's see if our country wants another go at that.

Apr 3, 2016

If ignorance is bliss, Donald Trump must be the happiest man on earth.

May 4, 2016

Trump says we're all going to say "Merry Christmas" again. So if a Jew refuses to say Merry Christmas, will Trump build a wall around him and send the bill to Israel?

May 5, 2016

American racists must be drinking Champale, or whatever racists drink, to celebrate Donald Trump as the presumptive nominee of the Republican Party. (White whine?) Racists probably think is our Reichstag Moment, the start of the Racist Renaissance. Soon white men will be in charge of everything again, and America will be "great" once more. To me, this is more like the moment when you flip on the light and discover that you have a real cockroach problem.

May 6, 2016

In Vietnamese "pho " means a certain kind of rice noodle. For breakfast you have two main choices, pho bò (beef noodle soup) or pho gà (chicken noodle soup). There are chopped Thai red chiles and Sriracha sauce to set it on fire. In my hood the two best places are right next door to each other. The chicken broth has been simmering in that pot for about thirty years now and just keeps getting better. Cost, 50,000VND, or $2 US.

May 13, 2016

Donald likes to come up with one-word nicknames for his opponents. This is a clue to how we should address him. Hillary should pick one and stick to it. I nominate"Weak Donald" or "Little Donald." Either one is true, either one should irritate the hell out of him and hasten his downfall.

May 26, 2016

David Brooks says "we" don't like Hillary because she doesn't have any hobbies and she's a workaholic. I think she should stop being so boring so that David Brooks would like her more. It would also help if she would stop being such a woman all the time.

May 27, 2016

Obama gave a marvelous speech at Hiroshima. He talked about the violence of war – all war. He talked about violence as a part of the human genetic and social code. He talked about the Japanese victims of the bomb – but then he also mentioned the Korean victims of the bomb, which is a subtle but unmistakable way of noting that Japanese aggression and atrocity was responsible for starting the war that led to the bomb -- and he mentioned 12 American POWs held in Hiroshima who also died in the atomic bombing.

I was in Ha Noi, watching English-language NHK coverage from Japan, which was, oddly, 10 minutes ahead of the "live" CNN and BBC coverage. The Japanese commentators emphasized the "inhumanity" of the bomb without referring to the war or Japan's role in starting it. They ignored Obama's reference to Korean victims of the bomb, but the BBC commentator noted that it made Prime Minister Abe's face twitch, and said no one in Japan would fail to understand what the President was saying.

After the speech, Obama greeted two very old men who survived the Hiroshima bomb. One of the men, Mori Shigeaki, burst into tears while speaking with the President, who immediately embraced the man, and steadied him until he regained his composure.

Now, imagine a President Trump in that situation.

May 30, 2016

I had a dream that the Republicans lost two elections in a row so they nominated the worst man in America to be President. Then I didn't wake up. Wait. Not the worst man in America. The second worst. The worst man in America is whoever sits at his right hand, muttering "Good idea, boss." And something tells me that ain't Melania.

May 1, 2016

Donald Trump called one reporter "a sleaze" and another "a real beauty" for asking hard questions about his bullshit lies about veterans. Personally I think he has early-stage dementia, and I wonder if anyone in the Republican Party is going to figure that out before the election.

Jun 2, 2016
[While I was living in Ha Noi, Obama made a wildly popular visit]

Bun cha is the dish that President Obama and Anthony Bourdain ate during the Prez's trip to Ha Noi. Many of the best restaurants in Viet Nam have one dish on the menu - you go there if that's what you want to eat, and to order, you sit down. "Bun cha" is a classic of Vietnamese, specifically Hanoian, street food. Obama delighted the locals by choosing to eat "street" instead of in a fancy restaurant.

For Bun cha, two kinds of pork - spiced ground-pork patties and pork belly - are grilled over charcoal until the edges are charred, then submerged in a sweetish broth containing fish sauce, rice vinegar sliced green papaya, Thai chile, and a lot of garlic. You submerge bundles of the "bun" (rice vermicelli) in this sauce and throw in herbs and greens like Thai basil, purple perilla, mint, and cilantro until you get it just the way you want. $1.50/serving. Obama liked his Bun cha so much he ordered a second serving (and a second local brew, Bia Hoi Ha Noi) ... with this qualification, he could now easily be elected President of Viet Nam if he wants the job.

Jun 3, 2016

Ten things Republicans hate about Hillary Clinton:

1. I don't know, I just hate her
2. She killed Vince Foster in Benghazi
3. Okay she didn't, but what if she did
4. If she'd been a good wife Bill would not have needed Monica
5. What was she doing in Benghazi anyway? Why wasn't she at home with Bill?
6. Man that voice just gets on my nerves, she reminds me of that woman boss I had
7. Where does she get off ?
8. I don't trust her because let's face it, you just can't trust her
9. Obama
10. If you just want to elect a woman there are plenty of great Republican women such as

Jun 6, 2016

"And My Feet Show It: A Poem by Donald Trump"

Look at my African-American over here!
Look at him!
Are you the greatest?
You know, it really doesn't matter what the media write
As long as you've got a young, and beautiful, piece of ass.
The beauty of me is that I'm very rich.
I've never seen a thin person drinking Diet Coke.
I was down there
And I watched our police and our firemen
Down on 7-Eleven
Down at the World Trade Center
Right after it came down.
I like people who weren't captured.
Tiny children are not horses.
I have a great relationship with the blacks.
I have always had a great relationship with the blacks.

Jun 7, 2016

The Republicans on Capitol Hill are miffed because they keep getting asked about Der Donald's latest racist tantrums instead of their beloved "issues." Note to future GOP leaders: nominating a fascist racist demagogue to lead your party may have repercussions.

Jun 20, 2016

I have been hearing voices in my head so I asked my psychiatrist about it. He said I don't have a psychiatrist.

Jun 21, 2016

The Republican Congress has found the solution to our problems: more guns! Guns now! Guns everywhere! Except at the Republican convention! Because guns make us safe! Except at the Republican convention! But guns in kindergarten are fine! And guns at gay nightclubs are fine! And guns in movie theaters are fine! And guns in the hands of terror suspects are awesome! Just not at the Republican convention! Because guns protect everyone, except Republicans at the Republican convention!

Jun 24, 2016

If by some chance this country decides to elect the Fuhrer of the Antiquated Hitler Youth, I'm going to Brexit so fast it will make your head spin.

Jul 9, 2016

I don't have too many Republicans among my Facebook friends. I have noticed that none of them ever defends Donald Trump. They support him but they don't defend him. They just attack Hillary Clinton.

It reminds me of my days growing up in Alabama. We called it "the Wallace Effect." Nobody in "nice polite white company" ever admitted to voting for George Corley Wallace back in the day, and yet somehow he always got elected.

I imagine lots of Hitler's supporters kept a low profile before 1933 and the Reichstag fire, too.

Any Republicans you know have anything good to say about Trump? Besides "he says what he thinks," which translates to "I am a racist just like he is."

Jul 11, 2016

Melania Trump came over this afternoon so we could work on her Republican National Convention speech. She wants to start out with "My fellow Americans" and I told her why I didn't think that would work. She asked if it would be okay if she sings the Slovenian national anthem if she does it in English and I said she would have to clear that with Mr Big. Her biggest concerns are Peace in our time and Making fur okay for women who can afford it. She's so excited - keeps saying she needs a new bikini for Cleveland. I didn't know what to tell her about the beach in Cleveland. The speech is good, though. Short, punchy. Apparently the Chanel suit and pink pillbox hat were just an idea, Melania doesn't get why everybody acted so touchy about it!

Jul 14, 2016

"I refuse to have a running mate. It's stupid. It's ghoulish. He's just standing there, waiting for me to die."

"It doesn't matter. You'll be #1. He will always be #2."

"I don't want a #2."

"You never have to see him or talk to him. He goes to funerals, that's it."

"Hitler never had a running mate. Why should I have to have a running mate?"

"Different system. He was running for Chancellor."

"I told you I want Sarah."

"You can't have Sarah. She'll take the spotlight away from you."

"Fat chance."

"Dad. It'll be okay."

"Thanks, honey. I wish you weren't my daughter."

"What?"

"Oh, you know what I mean."

Jul 15, 2016

I don't know who the hell Mike Pence is, but I'll bet you fifty bucks he is a very white man.

Jul 16, 2016

Just watched the full video of Donald J. Trump's VP announcement. It appears he has nominated himself to be his own Vice President. He talks about himself for 25 minutes and then this guy Pence wanders onto the stage and Donald gets the hell out of there like his ankles are on fire.

Jul 17, 2016

Official RNC Convention Schedule - NOT FOR RELEASE

Day 1

8 am Kid Rock welcomes attendees with national anthem
9 am Ivanka Trump, "Why My Dad Is So Frickin Awesome"
10 am Chip Trump "Dang Is My Dad the Coolest Er What"
11 am Buffy Trump "Things My Father Taught Me"
12 noon Pat Robertson "Gays Are Trying to Kiss My Lips"
1 pm Sadie Trump "I Sure Love My Cousin Donald"
2 pm Tim Tebow SCRATCH Other football player TBD
3 pm Melania Trump fashion show - 18+ NSFW
4 pm Scooter Trump "Donald Treats His Dogs Well"
5 pm Victoria Jackson "The NSA Got Me Fired from SNL"
6 pm Ted Nugent "Foreign Policy and the Future of America"
7 pm Track Palin performs "Smack dat Beyotch" from his new album "Track!"
8 pm Paul Ryan, "Vote For The Man Whose Name Is On the Poster"
9 pm Chuck Trump "Dad is A Mean MotherF (Shut Yo Mouth!)"

Day 2

8 am Paul Ryan, "Vote for the Man Whose Name Begins With a D"
9 am Ivanka Trump, "Things Dad Told Me I Left Out Yesterday"
10 am Tiffany Trump, "Kids You Never Knew He Had, Awesome Dad Part III"
11 am Ted Cruz, "My Endorsement Carries A Lot of Weight"
12 noon Pat Robertson "I Was Impregnated by Pot Smoking Gays"
1 pm Heffy Mae Trump "Donald Trump Is The Best Boss An Aunt Could Have"
2 pm Tom Brady SCRATCH Other football player TBD, pref. Negro
3 pm Rover Trump, "Alpha Dog on Fifth Avenue, a Love Story"
4 pm Some Mexican or Other Latino TBD
5 pm Miss Pittypat Trump "Cockatiels Have Gun Rights Too"
6 pm Mike Tyson, "Liberty, the Second Amendment, and the Downward Spiral of the Upwardly Mobile In Today's Consumerist Society"
7 pm Gov. Rick Scott "For the Love of Skeletor"
8 pm Gov. Chris Christie "Why Can't I Stop Crying: A Meditation"

9 pm Ivanka Trump, "You Better Get Used to Seeing me Here"

Day 3

8 am-9 pm Mike Pence, improv

Day 4

8 am-9 pm Donald J. Trump, improv

Jul 17, 2016

Donald J. Trump on '60 Minutes': "I think I am actually humble. I think I'm much more humble than you would understand."

Translation: I am so goddamn humble you can't believe it. You are too stupid to understand the depths of my humility. I am very, very humble. I am the most humble person in the world. I make Mother Teresa look like a braggart. I am the number-one humble man you will ever meet - number one in the world. I am so humble it will make you want to slap your wife. When it comes to being humble, you don't get any better than me. If Gandhi was alive he would tell you, Donald J. Trump is more humble than anybody including me! You want humble? Shut up!

Jul 18, 2016

Trump has just named his TV-nemesis Omarosa to be his director of "African-American Outreach." In other news, the Trump campaign named the Frito Bandito director of Mexican-American Outreach, that guy who played Fagin in the movie "Oliver" to head Jewish-American Outreach, and Mohandas K. Gandhi director of the Bureau of Indian Affairs.

Jul 18, 2016

If corporations are people, and wives are property of their husbands, then one of Donald Trump's most expensive current possessions, the former naked model Melania Knauss Trump, will be the lead speaker at the Republican National Convention tonight. I was hoping to watch but then I realized I would rather stick needles in my eyes. So that's what I'll be doing.

Jul 19, 2016

Melania Trump has just issued the following statement: "Four score and seven years ago, I asked not what my country could do, but instead I asked: Mr Gorbachev, tear down this wall! The only thing I have to fear is fear itself! I did not have sexual relations with that woman, Miss Lewinsky! There you go again! I will never lie to you. The buck stops here. Tippecanoe and Tyler too. In conclusion, the fundamentals of our economy are sound. Extremism in the defense of virtue is no vice! Love y'all! Night!"

Jul 19, 2016

Late last night on Pennsylvania Avenue:

Barack: What?
Michelle: Nothing.
B: No, what? Come on.
M: *Nothing.*
B: When you've got that look on your face, it is never *nothing.*"
M: I didn't do a thing.
B: Wait. Did Melania call you?
M: Noooo.
B: Did she call and ask you for help with her speech?
M: Nooo. Absolutely not. No way.
B: She did. She called you, and -
M: Not a chance.
B: Oh. You are such a --
M: Don't say it!
B: Can't wait to call Hill. She frickin owes you one.
M: Damn right she does.

Jul 19, 2016

The Trump campaign says they're not going to fire anyone for Melania's plagiarism. Does that mean they're really going to let Melania take the fall on this one? I see a very gold room in which an orange man is turning redder and redder while his beautiful wife weeps, furiously googling herself.

Jul 20, 2016

They're having an old-fashioned witch burning in Cleveland. "Lock her up!" chants the mob. "Guilty!" cries the prosecuting Governor. Magic Witch Hillary, who can fly through open windows at night and implant plagiaristic impulses in sleeping Slovenian beauties, is the focus of all their rage, now that the black man is soon to retire. Some of their leaders call for killing her, executing her. (The Secret Service is looking into that part.) Definitely a return to "traditional American values" as practiced in Salem, Mass. But at least, in Salem, the witch got a chance to prove that she was not a witch. They threw her in a pond and if she was a witch, she floated. If not, she drowned. I wish Hillary would appear in Cleveland and fly around the arena spelling out "Surrender Melania!"

Jul 22, 2016

So imagine a bunch of us sitting around the wasser-kooler in Berlin the morning after Hitler was proclaimed Chancellor. "I don't really like Weimar Germany," someone whines. "Yeah, I don't like those pant-suits." "And I can't stand that speaking voice of hers." "There's so much crime on the radio now, who's to say it's not the Jews' fault?" "You know, his children spoke very well, and I like that one's hair." "What can we do?"

Here's what we can do. We can save our country from those who want to take us - not back to the segregation and white-ruled society of the 1950s - but forward to a new kind of fascism with an All-American Branding Expert trying to restore "our place in the world."

You're either in this one or you're out. There's no straddling the fence. "Should I vote for the Fascist or the other one? Hmmm, let me decide, both our choices are so BAD!" No. They're not. They're not even close to the same kind of bad. If you think they are, you're either not listening or you're a fool. Or you think it's okay that your candidate is a fascist, racist, misogynist casino operator.

Jul 24, 2016

S: Mr Nixon?
RMN: Hmp. Yes?
S: Sorry to bother you, sir.
RMN: What is it?
S: There's a New Nixon, sir. Self proclaimed.
RMN: What? Somebody wants to be ME?
S: Yes sir.
RMN: Oh at last! I knew it! Pat? Did you hear that? (*crickets*)
RMN: I knew it was only a matter of time!!!
S: Sir? Just one thing.
RMN: What's that?
S: It's Donald Trump.
RMN: Donald Trump is the new ME?
S: Yes sir.
RMN: And it's working for him?
S: Uhm, yes. Appears to be. Blatant racist appeals, straight out of the George C. Wallace playbook.
RMN: Dammit! Why didn't I go that route? He's still a crook, right?
S: Oh yeah.
RMN: I tried to tell Haig - "in 20 years who will care? They'll be begging for a crook! Let em try 8 years of Ronnie Reagan!"

Jul 25, 2016
[WikiLeaks released transcripts of hacked emails by prominent Democrats]
Many of my Democratic friends are all bent out of shape about Debbie Wasserman-Schulz. I am more concerned about the source of the information that has everyone riled. Who hacked the DNC's

servers? (If they'd been private, like Hillary's, maybe that wouldn't have happened.)

What about reports that Vladimir Putin of the Trump campaign is behind leaking these emails on the eve of the convention? Is Debbie Wasserman-Schulz the real story here, or is it an obvious dirty trick from another campaign with the help of a foreign power, designed to divide Democrats at their convention?

Jul 26, 2016

It was 94 years ago that women were "granted" the right to vote, by the men who had kept them, quite often, as property. Today a woman was nominated as President by a major party for the first time. Let's see if they can do a little better than the men over the next 94 years. How about it, ladies? Congratulations to every woman who heard "no you can't" and kept right on going.

Jul 27, 2016

So now Donald calls upon the cyberespionage unit of the Russian government to hack Hillary Clinton and release her emails to the public. Isn't that sedition?

Jul 27, 2016

Trump's love for Putin is like Chris Christie's love for Bruce Springsteen: the pure, touching, unrequited love of a fanboy – would be kinda sweet if it weren't so pathetic.

Jul 28, 2016

Here's what I would say about Donald Trump if I were Hillary tonight at the Democratic National Convention: nothing.

Don't play his game. Tell us about the future, tell us how we are going to get there together alive and with some tiny bit of sanity intact. Tell us how you can help us stop wars and violence and madness in the streets. Tell us how you are going to help us educate the children. Don't talk about him. Talk about you, about us. We the people. WE the people. Not US and THEM. Talk about building bridges. Talk about the wall that some would seek to build, to keep the world and the future at bay.

And then maybe right at the end: "The Republicans have come a long way .... from Ronald Reagan wanting to tear down that wall, to Donald Trump proposing to put up a new one."

Jul 28, 2016

Trump now says he was being sarcastic when he suggested Russia hack Hillary Clinton. You gotta hand it to the guy, that is some Aaron Burr-level sarcasm.

Jul 28, 2016

"A man you can bait with a tweet is not a man we can trust with nuclear weapons." You tell him, sister.

She looked like the Angel Grandma and she stood up to the bully for girls, and boys, all over America.

Jul 30, 2016

This is how Donald Trump responds to the statement from Khizr Khan, the father of the fallen solder who spoke at DNC. "If you look at his wife, she was standing there," he said, on national television. "She had nothing to say. She probably, maybe she wasn't allowed to have anything to say. You tell me."

Trump is implying that because Khan's wife is Muslim, she was forbidden to speak. In fact, as she told MSNBC in a later interview, she was too overcome by grief at the death of her son.

As Patton Oswalt points out, this sentence gets funnier the more you read it: Trump said Khizr Khan "has no right to stand in front of millions of people and claim I have never read the Constitution."

Aug 1, 2016

In response to sharp criticism from Jesus H. Christ, Trump said, "I like people who WEREN'T crucified."

Aug 2, 2016

I was going to take a break from the endless string of Trump posts, but then he kicked a crying baby out of his rally, criticizing the crying baby's mother for not understanding how hard it is to give a speech when a baby is crying.

Aug 3, 2016

There once was an orange from New York
Who, in spite of the fact he's a dork,
Tossed his hat in the ring
(Thought he would be the king)
Now he's done, into him stick a fork.

Aug 4, 2016

I'm so glad Donald got rid of that bad baby. And the mother! Letting it cry! Not realizing how hard it is giving a speech when her baby is crying! That baby was a Muslim. That baby was Obama and was born in Kenya. That baby hates America and loves terrorists. That baby ate my dingo. That is one lousy baby. That baby did not invade Crimea. That stupid baby, why doesn't it go home. Infantile!

Aug 6, 2016

Paul Ryan and Don were dating. Then Don got mad. Then Paul said he hated Don. Then Don said he hated Paul. Then Paul said he loved Don. Then Don said he did not love Paul. Then Paul said he loved Don again. Then Don said, all is forgiven and please come home again.

How must it feel when you sell your soul to the devil and the devil goes, "no thanks?"

Aug 7, 2016

Dear World,

I Melania wish to notify Am trap in Giant Gold Ballroom please to help door lock, did NO plasherize spich of Michelle Obamma just 2 attractif girls thinking simlar thots Now no longer am I permit to go outside EVEN to swimpool or Spa. HELP Need $ or Gulfstream Jet this not a Joak –

Melania

Aug 10, 2016

Trump says, ""If [Hillary] gets to pick her judges, [there's] nothing you can do folks. Although, the Second Amendment people, maybe there is. I don't know."

This is the Republican nominee telling his supporters that if they don't like Clinton's choice of judges, they should get their guns and remedy the situation.

Aug 10, 2016

Here I am back in Ha Noi ... nice to be ... "home." There has been much progress in Viet Nam since the USA tried and failed to wipe the nation "off the face of the earth" (Barry Goldwater, 1964), We are allies now, and the Vietnamese are much better off than before. But they still have a one-party putatively Communist government in which dissent is stifled and everyone has to vote for the only party that is on the ballot.

I like our system in the USA. If you don't count Andrew Jackson, we survived 240 years without challenge from a homegrown racist demagogue....until now. We held up the torch of liberty to the entire world....until now. Forgetting for a moment the awful possibility of a Trump presidency, let's just stop a moment to consider the damage he has already done to our nation without being elected.

Aug 12, 2016

What our side most deplores about Trump, his racism and casual verbal violence, is exactly what Republicans love about him: "he's not politically correct." For them, "politically correct" is the ultimate putdown. For us, "racist" is the ultimate putdown.

One side thrills to the first open use of racist, violent language in a political campaign since the heyday of Jim Crow. One side deplores it.

There's not really any place for compromise here. Nothing to do with Hillary Clinton.

Giuliani: No 'successful radical Islamic terrorist attacks' in U.S. before Obama's presidency

Aug 15, 2016
Wait, Obama was mayor of New York City on 9/11?

Aug 17, 2016

Twas the 8th of November, and all through the house,
Paul Ryan was dreaming of holding the House.
The libels were laid by the chimney with care
In hopes that Trump's hopes were not so much hot air..
There were insults, attacks, killer punch lines, so clever,
Enough to make blood run from Megyn's wherever.

The racists were nestled all snug in their beds
While visions of slavery danced in their heads
Melania in her kerchief, and I in wig-cap,
Had just settled in for a gold-plated nap
When out on the web there arose such a clatter
I sprang from my bed to see what was the matter

Away to the window I flew like a flash
Then remembered my dome. Back to my room I dashed.
Re-covered, I turned to my concubine, Twitter,
Who listens to me when I'm feeling this bitter.
"Sad! Crazy!" I tweeted, "Pathetic! Insane!
You're about to elect an asshole with no brain!"

When what to my bile-bloated eyes should appear
But a little red sleigh and eight tiny reindeer
And then the reindeer quit to work for the Clinton campaign.

And then someone repo'd the sleigh.
And then I was alone in Atlantic City, what a hellhole.
And it was just me and Melania.
And I was a loser.
Loser.
Loser.
Sad!
And then I cried.

Aug 20, 2016

Freudian Trump berates Obama for being unable to "control" African-Americans. The last time white Americans "controlled" black people it was called Jim Crow. Before that, it was called Slavery.

It would make the Republicans happy if Obama could "control" "his people" half as well as Trump controls his white supremacists, Neo-Nazis and white nationalists.

Aug 23, 2016

The answer to "why do they hate her?" is "because she is a woman who wants to be powerful." Just as the answer to "why do they hate him?" is "because he was a black man who wanted to be powerful."

The most powerful response to hatred is love.

Aug 24, 2016

When Democrats criticize Trump, we tend to focus on the things he has actually done or actually said he will do - he'll deport 11 million people, Megyn's blood was coming out of her wherever, judges of Latino extraction can never be impartial, he sexually harasses his employees, he doesn't pay taxes and won't release his returns, he says Khizr Khan was a Muslim agent, etc etc etc

When Republicans criticize Clinton or Obama, they ignore the actual person. They go for wild conspiracy theories about things Clinton and Obama are secretly doing, have never done, have never said they will do. Like, Hillary Clinton is secretly dying. Obama is a secret Muslim. Obama is the founder of ISIS. Hillary wants to stealthily take your guns away. Hillary and Obama are in a secret dark conspiracy with Muslims and Mexicans to hand over America to the forces of Allah and Satan (same thing).

They cannot win on policy. Their only policy is Cut Taxes on the Rich and Hate People Not Like Me.

So they have to resort to fear, prejudice, conjuring, witchcraft, secret cabals, and Manchurian Candidates who represent comic-book levels of evil. Oh and by the way the Gay Muslim Marijuana Revolution To Destroy America will come to fruition in 2018, but please don't tell the Republicans.

Aug 25, 2016

Rush Limbaugh reveals that federally funded Lesbian Farmers are coming to take over your croplands. In all the years my family and I grew lesbians on our old homeplace, we neither expected nor received any kind of subsidy from the government! Indignant!

Aug 27, 2016

Sketch for first-act closer, "Trump! The Musical"

I'm walking back the walkback
I'm pivoting like hell
I'm saying what I said before in case you couldn't tell
I hated them in April, I hated them in June
I tried to stop in August but it seemed a little soon

I'm muddying the waters
I'm blurring every line
I'm going to make you love me if I have to break your spine

I haven't changed positions
Just changed the words I choose
I think the blacks will come around, what have they got to lose?
The Mexicans all love me - I know, I asked my maid
She said some stuff in Spanish but I'm not sure what she said

I'm muddying the waters
I'm broadening my base
I'm going to make you love me if I have to smash your face

I'm soft on immigration
Unless you want me hard
And if you want to build that wall, I'll build it till you're tired
I'll round up all the Muslims, and grant full amnesty
To anyone of color who will cast a vote for me

Aug 28, 2016

Sketch for mid-first act ballad, "Melania's Theme" - "Trump! The Musical"

I am wanting what I wanting
Never more to have no more
Give my love to him who needs me
Like the doorknob needs the door

I am all the way from nothing
I am something else to see
But the girl I been behinding
Is no little less than me

What can it be, you have to never know
Who can I me, if I can always go
Never to find the heart I said before
Always to winning
Always to rising
Sometimes to running
Who am I crying
Loooooove...

I am getting what I taking
Always here to soft your pain

Will be home when you come home, dear
Look, I bought some new Balmain

Aug 30, 2016
   When Donald Trump spends 15 months telling us America is a failed state, a bad place, a dangerous place, the Republicans nominate him for President. When a black quarterback offers one protest, Trump tells him to find another country.

Aug 31, 2016
[Trump visits Mexican President]

Overheard in the Palacio Nacional, Mexico City

"I love you people. Especially the Taco Bowls in the Trump Grill."
"Mr. Trump, we need to discuss your –"
"I had a woman who worked for me at Mar-A-Lago. Inez. Salt of the earth. Her English was fabulous."
"The reason you were invited today is that –"
"I love that movie 'Zorro.' Do you like that movie? Now there's a Mexican anybody could love."
"As the President of Mexico, I must insist that we address –"
"You people make the best guacamole. Can we get some guacamole? Maybe some of those chips?"

Aug 31, 2016
   What a day for Captain Littlefingers! First a visit to a country full of dark-haired mysterious women and some Mexican in a fancy office. The Mexican said stuff and the Captain said other stuff. Then a hop to Arizona where he got to say all the stuff he didn't say to the Mexican's face. What a day! Only 1 thing could make this better: takeout on the plane. Taco Bell? Not tonight. Enough Mexican for 1 day. Tonight KFC!

Sep 9, 2016
TRUMP: I want to blow up the moon with big rockets
CLINTON: Blowing up the moon is bad

PRESS: "Trump, Clinton Spar Over Moon Plans"

Sep 9, 2016

HILLARY: Half of Trump's supporters are racist
PRESS: Gaffe!
TRUMP: I think it's closer to 90 percent
RYAN: Donald, shut up

Sep 11, 2016
   I lived one mile from the World Trade Center on September 11, 2001. Every time I ride my bike past there, I stop and say hello to the people who died there. I knew two people who were there that day, so I say hello to them. And the other ones, the firefighters, the cops, the EMTs, and the normal people. I don't really believe in life after death but I always think I can feel people there.

Sep 11, 2016
[Hillary Clinton has the flu, stumbles at a 9/11 commemoration ceremony]

Discussion at Trump HQ about next tweet.
CONWAY: "Get well soon?"
TRUMP: "Loser"
CONWAY: "Speedy recovery?"
TRUMP: "Lock her up"
CONWAY: "Hope you feel better?"
TRUMP: "Benghazi"

Sep 12, 2016
   Hillary Clinton didn't announce she has walking pneumonia because she didn't want 24-hour cable coverage of it, so now she has 24-hour coverage of her decision not to announce it.

Sep 12, 2016
WOMAN GETS SICK

When a woman gets sick, she is showing her weakness
When a woman tries to conceal her sickness, and carry on with her work, she is showing her weakness
When a woman gets sick, she deserved to get sick
Women are not allowed to be sick
Women are always sick
Or pretending to be sick
But they are not supposed to tell anybody.
But they are supposed to tell everybody
Except who wants to hear from a woman who is sick
Because if she is sick she is weak.
Women are weak.

If a woman gets to feeling a little better and waves to the crowd
It is a different woman.
It is a body double.
It cannot be the same woman. The sick woman is weak.
The body double looks strong.

Sep 16, 2016
Trump Threatens Life Of Opponent Again. Yawn. Now back to live coverage of the "birther movement."

Sep 18, 2016
Almost time for the second rice harvest of the year in the paddies east of Ha Noi. It's peaceful but soon there will be a frenzy of activity. Did you know the Chinese put sticky rice in the mortar of the Great Wall of China? It made the mortar flexible in earthquakes, one reason parts of the Great Wall are still standing today.

Sep 19, 2016

Questions we're not supposed to ask:

    1. Is Trump assumed to be better on issues of "security" and "terrorism" because he is a boy not a girl?

    2. Is Trump suffering from early to mid-stage dementia? Does anyone among the 40 percent supporting him care if he is or not?

    3. How do you decide that making remarks that are "the textbook definition of racism" (Paul Ryan) are not disqualifying in a Presidential candidate? By what process do you reach that conclusion?

    4. Are we like those people in "Cabaret" who just went to the clubs and said well, those Nazis will never get in?

    5. If the answer to /4 is "yes," what can we do to change the end of this movie?

Sep 20, 2016

    Lester Holt of NBC is preparing a set of questions on topics he has chosen for the candidates in the first debate. To save time, I've provided a list of questions:

AMERICA'S DIRECTION

1. Mr. Trump, why is America going in the wrong direction and how will you correct that when you are elected on November 8?

2. Secretary Clinton, people just don't like you. It's been that way since you were born. Why?

ACHIEVING PROSPERITY

1. Mr. Trump, how can we achieve the kind of dazzling prosperity you exhibit in your daily life?

2. Mrs. Clinton, how many of your foundation's millions did you spend on makeup and hair?

SECURING AMERICA

1. Mr. Trump, we are not secure and we must be more secure, so can you please tell us how you will go about making us more secure, specifically by being manly and acting strong?

2. Mrs. Clinton, isn't national security one of the reasons a woman will never be elected President?

Sep 24, 2016
When Ted Cruz refused to endorse Trump in August, he said he was not just a "servile puppy dog." Today, when asked about his endorsement of Trump, he rolled over and thumped his tail twice on the floor.

Sep 24, 2016
Trump will invite Gennifer Flowers to the debate.

I once stood on a New Orleans hotel rooftop with Gennifer Flowers, singing "America the Beautiful" as the Fourth of July fireworks exploded over the Mississippi River, but that's another story.

Trump wants to be like Rhett Butler forcing Scarlett to wear the red dress to Melanie's house, to humiliate her. What he forgets is that Melanie treats Scarlett kindly, and shames the whole room.

Sep 25, 2016

TRUMP: Your wife's ugly & your dad killed JFK
CRUZ: Pathological liar, unfit to serve
TRUMP:
CRUZ: I love you with all my heart

Sep 25, 2016

Maybe Trump should develop some kind of signal for when he is trying to tell the truth. Like, he could wave both hands in the air. Or tug on both earlobes at once. That way we could stop what we are doing and pay careful attention to what he is about to say.

Sep 26, 2016

TRUMP BURNS HILLARY IN EFFIGY ON DEBATE STAGE
Clinton Puts Out Fire With Coughing Fit, Seen As Weakness

Sep 28, 2016

Cruelty is the act he does best. It's the quality that made him famous – a TV show that revolved around the moment when he fired and humiliated a different person each week. He enjoyed "firing" all those people and America enjoyed watching him do it.

Bullying a Gold Star family, bullying a woman who gained weight, bullying Mexicans, Muslims, refugees, and disabled people – these are classic expressions of racism, classism, and sexism, but the underlying quality uniting them all is personal cruelty.

His jokes, such as they are, are always made at the expense of others. His eyes light up when he thinks of a novel insult, or gets to revive an old one.

The serial adulterer crowed from the stage about how he was planning to say something "extremely rough" to his opponent, obviously something about her husband's adultery. But he stopped himself! He couldn't bring himself to do it!

One act of cruelty avoided for perhaps five minutes until he got off the stage and started congratulating himself for his forbearance. "Out of respect for Chelsea!" he crowed. Thus committing the very act of cruelty that he was bragging about not committing.

If elected, he will be the first openly, instinctively cruel man to be President of the United States.

The people who support him are cruel, too. They enjoy his cruelty as entertainment and look forward to his cruelty as policy. They support a man who built a career out of cruelty. These people are not nice, kind, or good people, no matter what they think of themselves. They're just like him -- they should be ashamed of themselves.

But we all know that's just not going to happen.

Sep 30, 2016

MELANIA: But Donald, I hungry
TRUMP: Spit it out
MELANIA: But you eat whole bucket of Extra Crispy
TRUMP: Spit it out
MELANIA: I not eaten since Labor Day
TRUMP: Your thighs are getting thick

Sep 30, 2016

Although my life has been varied and full of surprises, "check out sex tape" is not advice I have ever received from the nominee of a major political party at 5:20 am. Until today.

Oct 3, 2016

The last time Trump paid taxes, the future Melania Trump was seven years old.

Oct 4, 2016

If Trump is the sweaty salesman bobbing and weaving to try to sell you the car, Pence is the smooth manager who comes in at the end to declare that you're paying $800 for "undercoating."

Oct 4, 2016

Here's a helpful quiz: if I say "You're an idiot," which candidate am I voting for?

Oct 5, 2016

The Civil Rights Museum in Greensboro, N.C. declined Trump's request for a photo-op. So then his supporters threatened to burn down the museum. This is where we are right now in America.

Oct 7, 2016
[The infamous "Access Hollywood" audio is released, Trump brags about grabbing women "by the pussy"]

"I moved on her like a bitch" is just the kind of thing a President could say, then kids could memorize it and recite it at the beginning of class while facing the American flag. Belated thank you to the Republican Party for choosing a man who truly represents what your party has become. I didn't think you had it in you.

Oct 7, 2016

We're aboard Titanic, 23 minutes after striking the iceberg. Captain says we didn't hit hard enough, now he's turning the ship to make another run at it.

Donald J. Trump ✓
@realDonaldTrump

As I told everyone once before, Wiener is a sick puppy who will never change-100% of perverts go back to their ways. Sadly, there is no cure

5:34 PM · Jul 23, 2013

♡ 9.8K   💬 14.2K people are Tweeting about this

Oct 8, 2016

Titanic dead in the water, listing to starboard. Huge rush to throw the Captain overboard. Vice Captain huddling with junior officers. I hear the opening strains of "Nearer My God To Thee."

Oct 9, 2016

Three days ago Trump was running against Hillary Clinton. Now he seems to be running against the Republican Party. I hope Anderson Cooper asks him how it feels to be the first nominee in history abandoned by his party's leaders. That oughta get him going.

Oct 9, 2016

At the debate Trump:

1. Threw his VP under the bus
2. Threatened to jail his opponent
3. Confirmed he paid no federal taxes

Media calls it! Trump comeback!
Even Hitler didn't threaten to jail his opponents while he was running for office. He waited until he was Chancellor.

Oct 10, 2016

He rolled out the "put her in jail" line to distract the carnival from his pathetic attempts to make Billy Bush like him by revealing that he is the lowest lowlife horndog old scamp of a sexual-assaulting dominant male on the planet. That tape was like listening in on a direct feed from his id.

Oct 10, 2016

Paul Ryan: "I am not no longer nondorsing Trump, I am both thrilled and disgusted by the not not bad things he did or did not not not say, I am not not saying he should not be your President not, what I am saying not is that by nondorsing him, he is not not not the candidate you should not support, unless I change my mind, or find my spine, which is somewhere around here, I know because I saw it right after Chtulu spat it out on the floor." - from 'Profiles In Porridge'

Oct 11, 2016

If there isn't a law against a candidate for President directly colluding with and using hacked, stolen material provided to him by the Russian intelligence agency to influence the American election, could somebody please explain why not?

Maybe it won't be Hillary going to jail. Can somebody please put a hold on the cell next to Bernie Madoff?

Oct 12, 2016, 6:15 AM

I think Trump may have trouble getting dates after his little "Ode to Rape" on the bus with Billy Bush. So he's been working on his Tindr profile. Just in case Melania doesn't get that pained scowl off her face.

DeeJayTee - Hello, ladies! I'm a young 57, full mane of reddish, leonine hair, 6'1 and 205 lbs. I love working out, especially my thumbs. Looking for fine ass ladies who know a real man when they see one. If you are a 10, I will move on you like a bitch. I have so much money it's unbelievable. No one has more respect for women than I do. Love tall buildings, smokestacks, all things shaped like that, dunno why. (Locker-room banter warning) I want to give you a lot of my money (after you sign a few very unimportant papers) then I will grab you by the pussy and never let go. My hands are ENORMOUS so get ready. I am a star so you will let me do anything. I will treat you like a Queen - meaning if you cross me I will cut off your head and put it on a pike. Did I mention I am Very, very Rich.

Oct 13, 2016, 1:01 PM

I met Donald Trump at the American Booksellers Association convention in 1990. The occasion was a big party to promote the followup book to "The Art of the Deal." I shook his hand then stood about three feet away from him. His hair looked like a hairpiece. I remember hating the smug smile on his face and the way everybody was sucking up to him. He did not move on me like a bitch. Nor did he try to grab my pussy.

Oct 16, 2016, 12:24 AM

Might be faster if we just make a list of the women who have not been assaulted by Donald Trump.

Oct 19, 2016, 8:42 AM

If Hillary Clinton were actually the devil, Hell would have universal health care, tons of jobs, pre- and after-school programs for children of the damned, a serious effort to combat Infernal warming, free college education and a path to heaven for the deserving but wicked poor. And everybody would be clamoring to move there. Like Sweden but warmer.

If Donald Trump were the devil, on the other hand, Hell would be a much simpler place. Everyone there would be Donald Trump, and everywhere you went, there they'd be, crowds of Donald Trumps, bloviating, giving you their strenuous unanimous opinions about everything.

Oct 22, 2016, 9:24 PM

The Trump campaign started out as this huge joke that we all laughed at and ridiculed. Then he started doing well and the joke became a scary horror movie. Now the horror movie is turning out to be a parody of a horror movie but it's not funny any more and still kinda scary. I hope there is a big comic finish coming up and not a plot twist.

Oct 26, 2016, 7:27 PM

Originally I scheduled a trip to the USA for late October, thinking I might need to light up my torch and grab my pitchfork to keep the Mongols from storming the gates. As Fortuna's Wheel turned, though, the candidate for the Disaster Party is caught between tweeting blasts of disgust against the leaders of his own party and complaining about the parody version of himself on "Saturday Night Live." So I felt it was pretty safe to head back home to Ha Noi.

Oct 29, 2016, 6:02 AM

TRUMP: Burn the Capitol, call off the election, appoint me King, grab em by the pussy
COMEY: Somebody sent an email to somebody
CLINTON: I'm working on the transition

Oct 30, 2016, 6:38 PM

Trump: "People don't know how great you are. People don't know how smart you are. These are the smart people. These are the smart people. These are really the smart people. And they never like to say it. But I say it. And I'm a smart person. These are the smart. We have the smartest people. We have the smartest people. And they know it. And some say it. But they hate to say it. But we have the smartest people."

Even if you're a diehard Trump hater, you gotta give him this one just on style points.

Oct 30, 2016, 8:05 PM

Uh-oh, FBI Director Comey has decided to release the email he discovered on Anthony Weiner's phone. Brace yourselves, folks. I've got the text!

TOP SECRET HIGHEST CLASSIFICATION A++++

Dearest Comrade B. Hussein O.,

Time now for a little recap in my favorite medium, Email. There is absolutely no chance anyone but you and I will ever read this, so I feel free to speak the truth. Since I've been running for President for the last 16 years, I have thought it was wise to put my most damaging innermost thoughts into emails so that Republicans will have something to use against me when I run for office. I certainly hope they don't find this one - ha! Ha!

Hussein, you and I are well on the way to the Muslim takeover of the USA that we began plotting in that famous hotel room conference after the final primaries in 2008. Soon we will begin taking away the guns of all Republicans and giving them to super-predators so that we can consolidate our grip on the hellholes of our inner cities. The invasions of Alabama and Idaho are in the final planning stages. As I was saying to Vince Foster shortly before I killed him, "there is no way this plan can fail." I want to make sure that you have all the FEMA camps up and running by Nov 8, because the very next day, millions of our fellow Americans will find out what it is like to suffer under the dictatorship of me, the greatest criminal who ever lived.

I am certainly glad that we will win this election, and grateful that we were able to rig it so completely that it will appear to be a landslide. Thank you for sending secret mind-signals out to our supporters clueing them into the Great Awakening on Nov. 9.

Love to Michelle and the girls - see you on the podium on "Election Night!" Benghazi!

Allahu Akhbar,
Hillary

Oct 31, 2016, 10:01 PM

The New York Times says the Russians are seeking to disrupt the American election, "rather than" specifically help Donald Trump get elected.

Then where are the anti-Trump leaks?

Perhaps the Times doesn't understand that in a two-person race, if you leak the emails of only one side, you help the other. There have been no Wikileaks releases of Trump internal communications, only of the Clinton side.

We are through the looking glass when roughly half the electorate sees no problem in a hostile foreign power interfering in our elections as long as it benefits their party. Every day in every way, the GOP shows us they don't believe in ANY of their supposed "principles." They just want to win.

Nov 1, 2016, 6:32 AM

Trump used campaign funds to pay himself $13,000 to attend the ribbon-cutting at his DC hotel. I'd have gone for $1,000 and I would not have eaten all the Cheetos.

As for my plan to use Propofol to get me through Election Day, I am told it's all a matter of making sure you have an attentive physician on hand, undistracted.

Nov 2, 2016 9:45 AM

What is the main part of the word Female? EMAIL!

Why didn't it ever occur to me before now? Every time we've heard reference to "Hillary's email," they've been sending a subliminal message: "Hillary's female."

Nov 5, 2016, 7:26 PM

I was phonebanking with voters in NH and OH when one of my callees said the connection sounded funny. "I'm calling you on Skype from Viet Nam, hope the connection is not too bad." The lady said she was surprised to learn the Vietnamese are supporting Hillary. After I explained that I am an American who already cast his vote in Florida, she said, "I wouldn't vote for that man (Trump) if Jesus took my hand and tried to make me do it." I checked one voter off my list.

Nov 8, 2016, 2:58 AM

And so, the campaign that began with Trump declaring war on Mexicans ends with Sarah Palin's observation that "polls are for strippers."

All Hillary Clinton has to do is defeat Trump today, and she will go down in history as one of our greatest Presidents before she's even inaugurated.

Name a President who has performed a greater public service than sending that man back to his penthouse will be.

Nov 8, 2016, 9:17 PM

It's 10:15 a.m. in Ha Noi where I am and it's too early to drink. I want to go ride my bike but I'm afraid they'll give the keys to my house to a Trump supporter while I am gone. If you're still in line at the polls - stay there!

Nov 8, 2016, 10:48 PM

I was so very wrong. Sorry if I gave false optimism or encouraged complacency. I thought she had it in the bag. Can't watch any more CNN... if she pulls it out I'll find out later.

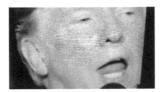

Nov 9, 2016, 3:42 AM

I know that I am supposed to respect the Presidency, but I have never lined up behind racism, xenophobia, sexism, or nationalism. And I'm not about to start now.

Hillary ran a great campaign. Trump went low. She went high. She lost.

Nov 9, 2016, 5:50 PM

Everybody on the Dem side is assuming our favorite position, the circular firing squad, to determine why Hillary lost.

The Republicans march onward, ever righteous in their quest to relieve the white man of his burden.

I'd say we lost because a coalition of groups that are united by being not-white and not-male is not yet strong enough to consistently beat a united white-power coalition working with every fiber of its collective being to maintain the power of white maleness in our society.

But we will be stronger next time. Time, demographics, and history are on our side. Trump and Putin are mortal, and so are all those who voted for them. Let's don't change who we are to try to imitate Republicans. Let's get to work on 2018.

Nov 10, 2016, 7:06 AM

Michelle Obama 2020. I mean, why the fuck not.

Nov 10, 2016, 8:30 PM

Turns out that Trump's very best investment of all was that slender night-table book of Hitler's speeches.

Nov 11, 2016, 9:31 PM

"Physically speaking, we can not separate. We can not remove our respective sections from each other nor build an impassable wall between them. A husband and wife may be divorced and go out of the presence and beyond the reach of each other, but the different parts of our country can not do this. They can not but remain face to face, and intercourse, either amicable or hostile, must continue between them.... Suppose you go to war, you can not fight always; and when, after much loss on both sides and no gain on either, you cease fighting, the identical old questions, as to terms of intercourse, are again upon you. This country, with its institutions, belongs to the people who inhabit it. Whenever they shall grow weary of the existing Government, they can exercise their constitutional right of amending it or their revolutionary right to dismember or overthrow it."

         - A. Lincoln, First Inaugural Address

Nov 12, 2016, 4:27 AM

On his tour of the West Wing, Jared Kushner asked how many of the White House staff would be leaving after the inauguration. Melania Trump says she will redecorate the White House.

Only remaining question is who plays Jethro.

Nov 12, 2016, 6:44 PM

I'm at that stage where you seek out documentaries about 1930s Germany and gesticulate wildly at the screen saying, to no one, "See? See? The EXACT SAME WORDS!"

What stage is that? It's past anger, and has nothing to do with denial. I think I am in the "Yes America You Did Choose* A Fuhrer" stage of grief.

I know some people will think it is excessive to call the president-elect a Nazi, but if he is going to appoint Steve Bannon, the nation's leading white-power media titan, as his chief of staff and script his campaign commercials directly from anti-Semitic Nazi screeds (global conspiracy of Jewish bankers) then I really don't think there is need to mince words.

Our first Nazi president. Wow! Crazy!

Sad.

The media and pundits who brought us Halloween in November are now advising us to Get With the Program and Support Our President-elect.

"Give him a chance," they tell us.

In his first real act as President-elect, Trump chooses the nation's most prominent white-power advocate, a rabid anti-Semite and propagandist, to be the director of his strategic vision. For some people, this is the final straw. For me, the final straw came on the first day of his campaign when he demonized an entire nation full of people.

I am not even sure he was legitimately elected. Is there some way we can we find that out before we give him the keys to the White House?

Maybe you can accept this man as President. I'm just not there. Can't imagine I ever will be.

Nov 15, 2016, 5:37 PM

Here is another installment of "Basically Impotent Rage." Please forgive me if you've already moved on.

The 2016 election began on December 12, 2000, when the Supreme Court of the United States ordered the State of Florida to stop counting the votes of its citizens, and awarded the state's electoral votes to George W. Bush.

When the Supreme Court decided (on a one-time basis, it declared) that certifying the result of the election was more important than counting all the votes, America took a step away from its own history. Voters had long held the illusion that they choose a President themselves. In 2000, for the first time since the election of Rutherford B. Hayes, that choice was taken out of their hands.

Old rules, said the court, no longer apply.

Bush v. Gore was a green light to those on the winning side. If you want to send squads of forceful young men wearing Brooks Brothers shirts to stop the legal counting of votes, the court said, we won't stop you. Since the old rules aren't giving your side the result you desire, the court said, go ahead and make new rules. We've got your back.

So, in 2016, when a candidate decided he could win by breaking all the rules – discarding the unwritten requirement that a person running for President behave with a certain decorum, seriousness, and intelligence, that he or she owes the country a reasonable facsimile of a democratic leader, and lip service, at least, to values of inclusiveness and fairness – Trump could be sure that the right wing would step up to help him.

The election of 2016 was, indeed, rigged. About this, Trump spoke the truth. Ronald Reagan started the rigging in 1987 when he abolished the Fairness Doctrine, allowing a thousand Foxes and Breitbarts to bloom. The Supreme Court gave a hard tug on the ropes with their decision to stop counting votes in 2000. Congressional Republicans added a few strings with their 2008 declaration that their only job was to make sure that Obama – and, by extension, the nation – failed.

Obama didn't fail. He succeeded, in spite of the tireless obstruction of the right. That a black President could succeed against their opposition drove the right nearly insane.

The most vivid way they could find to express this emotion was to elect Trump, a man who openly mocked most of the principles conservatives had long claimed to cherish.

They were assisted in this effort, according to intelligence agencies of the U.S., by the government of Russia. If proven, these acts constitute treason. But how can it ever be proven when the alleged traitors are being handed the keys to the government? Who's going to prove it? James Comey?

A house divided cannot stand. This election cannot stand.

Nov 16, 2016, 10:30 PM

You heard it here first: the Trump impeachment hearings will be a tougher ticket than "Hamilton."

Nov 17, 2016, 4:56 AM

It's bad enough they created their own dark fantasy world to live in, but now they're trying to make the rest of us go live there too.

Nov 18, 2016, 9:17 AM

Well, our racist President needs a racist Attorney General if he is going to dismantle civil rights laws in America. So Jefferson Beauregard Sessions III is a perfect choice.

Nov 20, 2016, 1:39 PM

Nixon: I am not a crook

Trump University settlement: Let's get this clear from the very beginning. I am a crook.

Time for the band to start practicing "Hail to the Thief."

Nov 24, 2016, 12:42 PM

I am thankful for publishers who publish my books and readers who buy them so that I can save my pennies and go to Washington D.C. on January 21, 2017,, to join the Million Women March (all feminists are invited) and help welcome in a new era of women fighting to achieve their innate power. See you there!

Dec 1, 2016, 5:04 PM

When an elder dies in Viet Nam, he or she is buried on the property where he lived out his life. Two years later, the family digs up the bones, cleans them, and buries them in the permanent grave. It's a hands-on process involving the whole family, who do all the labor themselves. (Along with ceremonies, dinners, etc.) For some reason this is a particularly busy season for the reburials. Almost every cemetery I pass on my bike has a family laboring away on a new home for an ancestor.

Dec 1, 2016, 8:58 PM

Trump keeps the press from barking by refusing to take questions, then tosses them chunks of red meat to make them SIT! STAY!

Dec 5, 2016, 10:36 PM

My brother Alan makes a point I've seen nowhere else. The Democrats now attacking the Electoral College system might want to consider that in 10 years, when Florida, Texas, Arizona, and Nevada have all moved firmly into the Dem column, the Electoral College will be our friend. We'll elect Democratic presidents forever. That's when the GOP will move to abolish it.

Dec 6, 2016, 4:52 AM

Ivanka is moving to DC but Melania is staying in NYC. I'm confused. Which one is going to be First Lady?

Dec 9, 2016, 9:45 PM

It's official: the CIA says Russia covertly hacked our systems to help elect Trump president. They succeeded at their goal.

What do we do now? Yes, it's a bigger scandal than Watergate, because it seems clear that Trump and/or his men committed treason. But in Watergate you had a Democratic majority in Congress to hold hearings and force the Supreme Court case that brought Nixon down.

Trump Committed Treason to Win the Election. And Hillary Clinton now leads the popular vote by 2.8m votes.

Dec 10, 2016, 10:11 AM

It's a democracy but you can't recount the votes because too many of the machines were broken and yes that's because the GOP cut funding for voting machines. So even if they stole the vote we'll never know because they also made sure the machines were broken and the law said that if machines were broken any recount could not proceed.

It's a democracy but the winner by 2.8m votes is the loser. And half the country is like, Okay fine!

It's a democracy but a Russian dictator hacked the system and probably installed his favorite, and not quite half the voting public are like, yeah Cool! Good!

As you can see I'm doing really well on my "getting over it" program.

Dec 11, 2016, 5:26 PM

Please stop telling me I need to "get over it" and support our President-elect. I have not supported him since he invaded Ukraine and I am not about to start now.

Dec 11, 2016, 10:09 PM

In the 1990s, when I lived in Costa Rica, I knew some people who were conned out of their life savings by some smooth operators of a Ponzi scheme. These "investors" were happy to reap their 12 percent monthly interest payments, and even bragged about it a little, though they had to have known there was something wrong with an investment providing that kind of unreal return, month after month..

Years later, after all their money was stolen, these people were still insisting the money was being kept for them in a safe account until it was okay for the swindlers to return it to them. This was after their swindlers had been arrested, convicted, served time, and released. They *still* believed.

Like people who voted for Trump.

Better to pretend it wasn't a con than to admit you were conned. That you supported a candidate actively working with a hostile foreign power to subvert our elections here at home. That's a reality you prefer to the truth of what just happened.

Dec 15, 2016, 1:54 AM

For the record, I don't think any of the Electoral College maneuvers will lead to anything more than the recounts in the three states did: the fix is in: the worst man in America will probably, illegitimately, take the office of President on Jan. 20. We haven't had a great man turn the office over to such a lousy man since Lincoln went to the theater. I will be in Washington on Jan. 21 for the Women's March on Washington. Ever since I first saw "Les Miserables," I've wanted to shake my fist at a tyrant, and now's my big chance.

Dec 25, 2016 7:34 PM ·

My dad prided himself on his ability to tie all the Santa Claus onto the car for the drive from Ohio to Alabama, then back again. In 1964, it all came sailing off the top of the car on the brand new interstate, I-65, between Calera and Jemison, our entire Christmas spread through the traffic lanes and systematically smashed to bits as we dodged into traffic to retrieve what we could. I don't think Dad ever tied stuff to the roof after that. From then on, we got small presents.

Dec 27, 2016, 6:06 PM

My friend Carrie Fisher died today. She was a second-generation movie star, and once told me that made it hard for people to talk to her. "They expect me to be a bitch because that's what I was raised to be," she said. She was not a bitch, but she had a truly cutting and original wit. She loved startling people with the sharpness of her rapier. I bet you can remember her big line in her first big role, opposite Warren Beatty in "Shampoo." She wanted to shock us, startle us, amuse us, entertain us. She was wonderful.

Anyone who ever knew her would tell you Carrie Fisher was smarter and funnier than anybody. "I tell my younger friends that no matter how I go," Carrie wrote, "I want it reported that I drowned in moonlight, strangled by my own bra."

Dec 29, 2016, 9:42 PM
[Debbie Reynolds dies suddenly, one day after her daughter Carrie]

I knew Carrie, and although she did love Debbie, don't you think for a second she wouldn't have a lot to say about her mother upstaging her this way. Go back and read "Postcards from the Edge" for details.

Mother and daughter were joined at the hip. They were a team. Often a fractious team. From the outside it may have appeared that Debbie took care of Carrie, but the reverse was just as often the truth. I think anybody who knew them is not really surprised that one wouldn't stick around without the other. They both brought a lot more joy to the world than they took from it.

2017

Jan 2, 2017, 8:29 PM

Only a schizophrenic nation could elect Barack Obama - twice - then turn around and elect Donald Trump. This nation needs electro-convulsive therapy. And boy are we about to get it.

Jan 5, 2017, 5:47 PM

Q. How many Trump supporters does it take to screw in a lightbulb?
A. There is no lightbulb.
Q. Yes. There is a lightbulb. I am looking at it.
A. No you're not.
Q. Yes. See that? It's a lightbulb.
A. No it's not. You are looking at a Trump Torch.
Q. *sigh* Okay. How many Trump supporters does it take to screw in a Trump Torch?
A. (smashes lightbulb) Won't be needing this.

Jan 5, 2017, 11:13 PM

I want gridlock. Sweet, sweet gridlock. I want the Democrats to tie the Republicans in knots. I want them to oppose everything and file suit against anyone who opposes their opposition. I want a Democratic Party that stops at nothing to stop Donald Trump in his tracks. I want an opposition that allows absolutely no "progress" to take place over the next four years. Status quo is fine. Bring me gridlock. Delicious, nutritious gridlock. GRIDLOCK, PLEASE.

In my reading about the early days of Nazi Germany, I found that one pernicious effect of the Hitler regime was that most artists stopped working. "It was too distracting, too diverting," one intellectual said. "Every day there was something new you had to oppose. You couldn't get your work done. It seems trivial but it wasn't."

So we need to practice resistance in both senses of the word: not just 1/ the act of opposing something, but also 2/ the ability not to be harmed by something, as in resistance to a cold.

It may not seem important for artists to get their work done, but to me it's more important than ever. We can't let them stop us from attempting to make our art, whatever it is and how trivial it may seem among the flood of politics..

Jan 11, 2017, 9:39 AM

He has nine more days of being the worst President-elect in American history. He becomes impeachable at 12:01 pm on January 20, 2017.

You know he will be Unpresidented. It's just a matter of time.

Jan 14, 2017, 4:24 AM

I should have been a pair of ragged claws,
Scuttling across the floors of silent seas.
Filled with bile, giddy with natural poison,
Scuttling up the leg of the golden table,
Scuttling past the wrist of the angry beauty,
Past repetitive motions of the computer whiz,
I should have run across the table to
Dive with all my funky fatal contamination
Into the soup of the one with tiny fingers.
BUT
Shoulda
Woulda
Coulda....
So maybe
I should have been a bucket of KFC
Extra
Crispy

Lousy with cholesterol, dripping with hemlock,
Soaking my oil into the soft cardboard bucket
Waiting to perform sacred duty.

Jan 15, 2017, 6:15 PM

If you live in a city, or dream of living in one, it's because you gravitate to other people. You take energy from having a buzz of other people around you: humanity as a beehive. You are more inclined to vote Democratic because you meet more kinds of people every day. People from every walk of life.

If you live in the country, or in the suburbs pretending to be the country, it's because you'd rather be in the wide open spaces. You take energy from the wildness of nature and the freedom to shoot a gun at a bird on your forty acres, if that is what you want to do. You are more inclined to vote Republican because you don't really want a bunch more people flooding in to occupy the land you love.

Like many people, I have a country side and a city side. When I'm in the city I'm dreaming of the beach. On the beach I think about Manhattan.

2000 was a tie. The countryside won in 2004. The cities were victorious in 2008 and 2012. The countryside squeaked by in 2016.

Jan 20, 2017, 2:24 PM

Let me be among the first to say, Impeach president* Trump! Today it begins. Get him out of the People's House.

Jan 20, 2017, 9:36 PM

I am a butthurt snowflake feeling so excited to be among hundreds of thousands of liberal women tomorrow. I aspire to be Nasty and I hope they will let me be Nasty right along with them.

Jan 22, 2017, 7:01 AM

About the Women's March on Washington:

1/ The Metro system in DC was completely overwhelmed. Train after packed train whizzed through stations without picking up passengers. It took 2 ½ hours to travel from Capitol South to Crystal City, normally a 15-minute trip.

2/ The march organizers did their best, but the crowds were much larger than they expected. The crush of humanity on the streets beside the Mall was so thick at some intersections that about 30 people fell out near the medical tent where I volunteered for the afternoon. Many people made the observation that if the crowd had not been so kind and good-humored, it could have become a nightmare. It didn't.

3/ There were apparently zero arrests in a gathering of around 1,000,000 people.

4/ Mothers with daughters, sisters linking arms, trans folks, men, children, grannies, grandpas. All of them smiling and hugging and cheering and chanting. Take a note, Trump.

5/ Funniest comment I heard all day, related by Chuck, a DC cop: Lady wades up to through crowd, stretching literally miles in all directions, and asks, "Is this the march?" He said, "No ma'am, go four blocks west and look for the people, that'll be the march." Then he smiled and told her that yes, this was the march.

6/ I think a lot of the marchers have been in a funk since Nov. 8. By the end of the day, everyone I saw looked exhausted and exhilarated.

7/ There were tons of porta-potties but the women organized this one themselves so there could have been a lot more. Can't blame us males for this one.

8/ Taken with the Sister Marches around the country and around the world, this was the largest demonstration in the history of America. And that was only Trump's second day in office.

9/ 2018. 2018. 2018. 2018. Repeat after me. 2018.

10/ It was one of the great privileges of my life to march with these strong and nasty women. Thanks to everyone who was kind to me all day long. Now we know the opposition is real and we ain't going nowhere. As Mother Pollard of the Montgomery bus boycott said, "My feets is tired but my soul is rested."

Jan 25, 2017, 6:02 AM

I arrived back home in Ha Noi just in time for the beginning of Tet, the festive celebration of the Lunar New Year made famous by a certain offensive in 1968. The whole country shuts down for a week as the cities empty out - everyone goes back to his or her home village to celebrate with family and friends. This morning the traffic was crazy. Tomorrow is New Year's Eve and you have to get everything ready at home.

Seemingly half the people in Ha Noi were toting these enormous fruit-laden kumquat trees (or blooming peach trees) on the back of scooters and bicycles and every vehicle imaginable. The kumquat signifies the many generations living together in the family - the fruit is the grandparents, the flowers are parents, and the buds and green leaves are children.

The kids anxiously wait for "Li Xi," or "lucky money," which is what good children get in red envelopes on New Year's Day.

Jan 27, 2017, 9:07 AM

Trump's first week in office was the worst week for an American President since Richard Nixon's last week in office.

His first approval rating in the Quinnipiac Poll is 36 percent. In his eight years as President, Obama's worst rating in that poll was 38 percent. He's crashing so fast we'll have to call him Herr Hindenburg.

Jan 28, 2017, 5:55 PM

Imagine you have spent the last six or eight years getting all your papers in order to relocate to the land of freedom, the land of your dreams, the United States of America. At last after all the years and bureaucracy and expense you will be allowed to flee the repressive war-torn nation of your birth and fly toward the Statue of Liberty with her torch held high.

Imagine you get off the plane with your legal visa and all your carefully-gathered papers, only to be informed that the laws of the United States changed while you were in the air.

Imagine being pulled over to one side by a officer of the Immigration and Naturalization Service, and asked, "Sir, ma'am, what religion do you practice?"

You don't have to imagine any of this any more. It started happening for real last night in the airports of the United States of America.

Jan 31, 2017, 4:29 AM

Trump has put Steve Bannon in charge of the national security of the United States of America. I swear, I did Nazi that coming.

Feb 1, 2017, 9:40 PM

EXCLUSIVE: unedited transcript of Trump call with Australian PM Malcolm Turnbull.

DJT: Hey what up, is this the guy in charge of Austria?
Malcolm Turnbull: Well actually, Mr President, it's Australia.
DJT: I can never keep track of you two, which is the one that went with the Hitler folks early on?
MT: Austria
DJT: And that's not you?
MT: No
DJT: Okay well somebody is lying here and I know it's not me.
Unidentified Aide: He's the Prime Minister of Australia, sir.
DJT: Why would I be talking to Australia? Do I even have a hotel there?

MT: No
DJT: So I hear you're trying to dump a bunch of terrorist refugees into the US of A
MT: Actually, sir, the US has already agreed to take 1,293 -
DJT: Forget it, loser. Take a hike.
MT: I beg your pardon?
DJT: You're a losing loser from Loserville. Got that? I'm done. If you don't like our country GET OUT.
MT: Mr President -
DJT: Dammit, Steve! This is the worst call I had to make all day. *click*

Feb 3, 2017, 11:00 PM
    Some federal employees have reported confusion in the ranks on the Executive Branch's expressed preference that women who work for the President ought "to dress like women." I tried posting some portraits of the First Lady as a guide to acceptable woman-like dress around the Oval Office, but Facebook suspended my account for pornography.

Feb 8, 2017, 5:04 AM
[Elizabeth Warren is censured for reading a letter from Coretta Scott King on the floor of the Senate]
    The white men found it disrespectful of the white woman to use the black woman's words to question the motives of the white man. They voted to make her shut up and sit down, to stop her in the middle of her speech. Speaking against racism is now officially deemed conduct "unbecoming a Senator."
    "She was warned," the white man said. "She was given an explanation. Nevertheless, she persisted."
    Damn right. She persisted. She will persist. And she will outlast you.

Feb 12, 2017, 5:42 PM

There's a rumor going around that Sarah Palin will be the Ambassador to Canada. Word is, she's resisting taking the job because of the very real challenge of learning to speak Canadian.

Feb 12, 2017, 10:45 PM

He's been richly impeachable since his first minute in the Oval Office. *Emoluments.* He's only added to the list since that day.

The only thing standing between him and impeachment is the Republican Party. They have demonstrated repeatedly that they have neither principles nor testicles. They will not suddenly develop principles, or testicles.

But one of these days they will recognize that he is a liability to them. The worst mistake they've ever made. And then he's gone. Faster than Paul Ryan fleeing a gay porn theater.

Feb. 14, 2017 4:54 AM

Flynn is gone. Now he will either sing like a bird or fly home to his other employer, Putin.

The DOJ (Sally Yates) informed Trump and Pence a month ago that Flynn was compromised by his Russia contacts.

Trump and Pence took action. They fired Sally Yates.

Then they lied and lied, and let Flynn continue to pass on information to his Moscow friends. Whatever Putin has on Trump, it is BIGLY. Whatever Flynn knew, Trump knew. Pence knew. They're criminals. Lock 'em up.

Hillary Clinton repeatedly raised the subject of Trump's compromising Russia ties during the debates. The New York Times and most other press bought all of Comey's lies, and downplayed the Trump story in favor of stories about Clinton's emails. Now they're all trying to make up for lost time. And that's good. But let's not pretend this is new.

Feb 19, 2017, 10:16 PM

He has been in office exactly one month. I don't know about you, but that felt like the longest month of my life. I need this man to get out of my head, off my screen, and out of the People's House.

Feb 21, 2017, 4:35 AM

Hey I know, you guys! Let's all send rope to the White House. As a gift. To make sure he has enough.

Mar 1, 2017, 9:21 PM

One of my favorite moments of New Orleans' Mardi Gras is midnight on Fat Tuesday, when the celebration officially comes to an end. The police start at the Canal Street end of Bourbon Street - in recent years preceded by the aggressive Christian fundamentalists who come to harass gay people in the name of Jesus - and sweep the street clear of partiers, followed by the mounted police, followed by the miracle workers of the sanitation department. Revelers gather to cheer the police and street-sweepers as they proceed the length of the street.

By early next morning, there are drunks passed out all over the Quarter, many of them tagged with ashes on their foreheads, denoting a stop by the Cathedral on their way to slumber....

Mar 2, 2017, 10:00 PM

Maybe my life is just too empty of events, but I do believe I would remember every conversation I ever had with Russia's top spy.

Mar 4, 2017, 8:48 PM

New lines by Edgar Allan Trump –

In my tower above the city,
After days of deep self-pity,
As I nodded and began to napp,
Suddenly there came a tapp.
A visitor began to rapp,
Rapp as I tried to napp alone.

"'Tis Barack," I said and groaned,
"Who tapps upon my telephone –
Very unfair!" did I then moan.

Mar 6, 2017, 4:52 PM

The Star-Spangled Bannon

O say can you see by the phone's pearly light
What the president said to Melania, screaming:
"Who's responsible for my most unhappy night?"
Through the Twitterverse sails his incredible meme-ing
And I once had red hair
A red tie down to there
My Dad always said I was not a great heir.
O why will I never be my father's fave?
If I can't win your love, it's your hatred I crave.

Mar 6, 2017, 5:55 PM
 Great news on the GOP plan to replace Obamacare. 1. You get to die quickly in the comfort of your own home. 2. You get to keep your illness!

Mar 8, 2017, 1:27 PM
 Almost every problem in human history started with a stupid man who thought too highly of his intellect.

Mar 9, 2017, 8:17 AM

I should have been a pair of ragged claws
Lying in wait
On a plate
At Mar-A-Lago

Mar 10 2017, 4:43 PM

Sending in my taxes. So relieved to have worked hard all year in order to pay .00125 percent of the cost of one day of keeping Melania away from the man she detests almost as much as I do.

Mar 11, 2017, 2:31 AM

All over America tonight, little boys are dreaming that one day they may grow up to be craven, greedy, mean, and foul-mouthed enough to become President of the United States.

This is the future the Republicans wanted for us.

Mar 13, 2017, 10:59 AM

Kellyanne Conway suggests that Obama spied on Trump by turning a microwave oven into a camera.

I've had a frank and open discussion with my kitchen appliances about espionage. It got a bit emotional at times.. The microwave keeps muttering about civil liberties, although most of the muttering is in Chinese, so hard to interpret. The electric teakettle is complaining that the hand-held blender has been speaking with Russian operatives while I'm not home. The refrigerator has been spreading nasty rumors about the TV in the bedroom, which in turn claims the fridge leaves its door wide open when we're all asleep. The noise-cancelling head-phones claim they couldn't hear a thing - they're faking! - and the CD player just sulks and says it is "obsolete technology."

We worked it all out but after all the rumors, we discovered that my Sonicare toothbrush was texting pictures of my tongue to its control in Berlin.

Mar 14, 2017, 6:43 PM

The picture I see is that Trump was beyond broke when he took office - in hock to Putin and the Russian mob - and his entire 'presi-dency' is an elaborate loan-repayment plan. With occasional drop-bys from Mikhail, the guy who never sounds threatening, but has this way of holding a metal pipe in his hand and softly slapping his palm with it.

Mar 17, 2017 ·6:54 PM

Some Limericks

His case of mental diarrhea
Will take us to war with Korea.
Good thing his mouth
Cannot tell north from south:
"Don't invade whichever one makes Kia"

Confronted with Angela Merkel
Trump decided to act like a jerkel
Extended no courtesy
Needn't be her to see
Some jerks just jerk in a circle

There once was a golfer named Don
Who spent more time off-job than on.
With his wife in the Tower
He won't spend one hour
But show him nine holes and he's gone

It's hard to be nice to Melania
When you've got all this pressure upon ya.
Didn't think I'd be knighted
But whoa, wait! Indicted?
I just learned to pronounce *"do svidanya!"*

Mar 23, 2017, 11:48 PM

Republican Pancakes

1 c. cornpone
1 c. water from Flint, Michigan
½ c. alternative flour (may use cement powder)
1 c. the horse you rode in on

1 c. melted snowflakes
2 eggs, fertilized and granted immediate citizenship
1 tsp. free-range malarkey
2/3 c. poorly disguised racism
4 oz artisanal Cheez Whiz
1 tsp. Liberal tears

Stir all ingredients together and cook on griddle until half-baked.

Mar 27, 2017, 4:52 AM

One out of every 3 days he's been 'president,' Trump has visited a Trump-branded property. And billed us for it.

If you traveled for business, stayed at your own home, and billed your company for it, you'd be fired for malfeasance. But he's just the "president."

Apr 3, 2017, 5:50 AM

The village of Thôn San is like an island in the middle of an ocean of rice. It was so peaceful this morning. Easy to forget that Nixon and Kissinger bombed the levees nearby to try to eradicate the "fighting will" of the villagers. I guess no one ever told them the people of Thôn San have been repelling invaders quite effectively for 1,000 years.

Apr 3, 2017, 7:00 PM

Q. How long does it take Donald Trump to screw up a light bulb?
A. You heard me.

Apr 4, 2017, 6:48 PM

One curious requirement of being a modern racist is to insist that you're not. "I don't have a racist bone in my body" is the number one tell. Comes right before the coded (or uncoded) racist statement.

Anyone who grew up in the South knows that we're all racists. Not just Southerners, the whole country. (And a large part of the world.) We were raised that way. We have to fight every day to overcome this burden. Not being a racist is impossible. Fighting the tendency is the only solution I know. (That and education, but oh well.)

Apr 5, 2017, 10:30 PM

The New York Times corrects an error that is quite understandable in context.

Correction: April 5, 2017
Because of an editing error, an earlier version of this article misidentified Ivanka Trump as President Trump's wife. His wife is Melania. Ivanka is one of his daughters.

Poynter @Poynter · 3h
NYT corrects: Ivanka Trump is the president's daughter, not his wife:
nytimes.com/interactive/20... pic.twitter.com/j4H4MlXali

56   185   242

Apr 10, 2017, 9:51 PM

This morning from the seat of my bicycle I witnessed a small transaction. A very old man was purchasing a single red rose from a young vendor on the street of a village near Ha Noi. I imagined the possibilities...

The rose was for a girl about the age of the flower-vendor -- his granddaughter, perhaps, or someone whose birthday is today.

...Maybe he is buying it for his love, who is aged as well, and is waiting at home for the surprise he will bring her.

...Maybe his love isn't here any more. He'll carry the rose over to the place where she's resting now. He'll leave it for her, knowing how she always liked roses.

...Or maybe he's just a man who likes to have a fresh flower on the little table beside his bed.

I hope someday I get to be ninety so I can mystify someone by buying a single rose.

Apr 11, 2017, 10:38 PM
Canadian tourist in Ha Noi café: "What is up with all these weird squirrels without bushy tails?"
Me: "Those aren't squirrels."

Apr 17, 2017, 11:56 PM
Waking up every day with Trump as president* is like opening the fridge to find that the milk is always spoiled, every damn day, no matter how many times you throw it away.

Apr 21, 2017, 7:37 AM
Sarah Palin, Ted Nugent, and Kid Rock just spent four hours at the White House with Trump. There haven't been that many idiots gathered in one room since the last time Trump dined alone. (Apologies to the spinning ghost of JFK)

May 1, 2017, 11:00 PM
Trump's fans don't care if he does everything wrong or if he had the help of Vladimir Putin to "win" the election. This is the hardcore 38 percent who love him for his incompetence, venality, and ignorance, because it confirms and reflects their own. The result of thirty years of Republicans trying to starve public education is this: Idiocracy.

May 4, 2017, 6:27 PM
There's something weird in the corn flakes. Almost half this country has lost its freaking mind. We've gone from "Yes We Can" to "Die Liberal Die."
They love it when he lies to us. Don't they realize he's also lying to them?

May 16, 2017, 1:38 AM
Let's sort this out: Trump leaked to the Russians so the Russians wouldn't leak the tapes of the Russian hookers leaking on Trump.

May 16, 2017, 6:25 PM

Nixon was forced to resign because he was heard on tape discussing the *possibility* of firing the FBI Director.

Trump blatantly told Comey in February to drop the Russia investigation. This goes far beyond what Nixon did to cause Republicans in 1974 to return articles of impeachment. But I suppose we can't expect the same from today's GOP.

Comey noted in February that Trump obstructed justice, but Comey didn't do anything about it or tell anyone. Guess he was all worn out from preventing Hillary Clinton's election.

May 18, 2017, 12:03 AM

Trump whining to graduates of the Coast Guard Academy: "No politician in history — and I say this with great surety — has been treated worse or more unfairly."

Tell that to Mussolini. He ended up swinging by his feet beside his mistress.

May 21, 2017, 4:47 AM

Dear World,

Yes we know he is naked, yes we are perfectly aware that he has sallied forth wearing no clothes, I mean no clothes at all. We apologize for asking that you compliment him on his splendid new robes, his most royal and deserved red robes, the greatest and finest robes ever draped around the shoulders of a leader - better, by far, than the robes of Obama - but we do ask, most humbly, that you flatter and coo and cajole, tell our emperor how marvelous a countenance he presents to the eye, how accomplished and pleasingly intelligent he appears in his fine new red robes, the unsurpassed luxury of the soft ermine collar, the fabulous twinkle of the bejeweled sash. The man is naked. We know he is naked. We can see with our eyes. We are perfectly aware. Please, just send him back here. And try not to let him near your women.

With Love, a goodly portion of the USA

May 31, 2017, 10:16 PM

My liberal friends won't like this, but I must observe that yesterday was the day Donald Trump finally became the Presfefe.

Jun 25, 2017, 7:49 PM

Trump is Miss Daisy with dementia. He'd rather smash the car into a wall than let the smart dignified black man drive one more minute.

Jun 28, 2017, 11:10 PM

Oh lordy, if only this was a real Witch Hunt. We could find a Good Witch to break the evil spell and send the Humbug back to his Tower. And then the Flying Monkeys could make fun of him and throw bits of food at him all day long.

Jul 2, 2017, 7:53 PM

Thesis: God is a woman with a twisted sense of humor, like Bette Midler, or Cher, and this past year is Her way of making sure the USA never elects a man to the presidency again. Men have had 10,000 years to screw up civilization. Women can fix it in 10 years. Backwards. And in high heels.

Jul 3, 2017, 6:05 PM

Donald was so excited about his upcoming date with Vlad that he could barely speak. "What shall I wear?" "The red pinafore or the dotted Swiss?" "Do you think he'll like a girl better with a permanent wave?" He stayed up late last night writing in his diary - the one with the lock on it, and the secret little key. "Mrs. Donald Putin," he wrote. "Mrs. D. Putin. Mr. and Mrs. Vladimir Putin, Esq." Oh, and what if Vlad should ask him to dance! He would love it but sometimes he felt so clumsy, the big feet and the tiny hands. What if he said something silly, in his schoolboy Russian? Would the older boy mock him? Would he notice, and shyly forgive the error?

Jul 7, 2017, 1:48 PM

TRUMP: You hacked our election!

PUTIN: Nuh-uh
T: You didn't?
P: Nope
T: But we PAID!
P: lol

Jul 12, 2017, 3:33 PM
Trump is mad because he saw people on TV saying he watches too much TV.

Jul 26, 2017, 10:48 PM
O William Randolph Hearst you rich dead man, you, deader than the business that riched you up richer than Gates, Musk, or Zuckerberg! You owned a whole kingdom and built a magnificent palace, but on the spine of its great brown bear of a mountain your palace is no bigger than a flea.

Jul 30, 2017, 6:53 AM
I was driving across the country from San Francisco to New Orleans. East of El Paso, the sign said pull over for "inspection." I thought it quaint and a bit aggressive that Texas is now keeping California fruits out of Texas after years of having it the other way around. Turns out they weren't inspecting for fruit, or insects. They were searching for those who come here to pick the fruit. They asked if I was a US citizen. I said Yeaaaaah, what's it to ya, Bub. They dragged me from the car, rending my garments. They tattooed impertinent slogans upon my breastplate. They hurled calumny at my person. They questioned my veracity and slandered my forebears. They said my dog was ugly and my cat was shallow and untrained. They called me a fop, a fussbudget, a bounder. They insinuated and rebuked. Then they looked at my passport and laughed at how bad the picture is, and they let me go. Welcome home to America!

Aug. 4, 2017 8:00 AM

Be sure to bring your ticketless ticket, because you can't get on board the train without your ticketless ticket. Or, as it used to be known, your "ticket."

Aug 9, 2017, 10:35 PM

You have selected: *Thalys Ticketless*
Ticketless: fast, simple and convenient.
You will receive an email confirming your order. Each ticket will be sent seperatly to the email adresses entered.
The date of departure, Ticketless ticket you received by email or your Thalys TheCard card must be shown.

The air is unbreathable some days. The city teems like an anthill with too many ants. The traffic is hilarious, stupid. Nobody looks where they're going - they just go. And yet, for all this, and because of all this, Ha Noi is just sublime.

Aug 15, 2017, 7:39 PM

Normally I can't watch him, but you really need to see the "president" of the United States making his spirited defense of the Nazi and KKK protesters seeking to protect statues of Robert E. Lee and Stonewall Jackson, who fought to destroy the United States. His defense of the Confederacy seems truly heartfelt.

Aug 17, 2017, 11:03 PM

One obvious argument against the concept of white supremacy is that Donald J. Trump is white.

Aug 18, 2017, 6:35 AM

Why don't we just tell Trump that most of the best Presidents resigned at the end of their first year in office, having done everything they could possibly do given the dysfunctional nature of the government, and that the ones who resigned before Christmas get double salary for the whole four years they would have served, and that the ones who quit before Thanksgiving get statues built of them in any New Jersey city of their choice, the kind of statue that laws are passed to protect, so that no one can come along later and take the statue down?

Aug 18, 2017, 11:19

Trump can give up Steve Bannon, but like Heath Ledger trying to quit Jake Gyllenhaal, he can't give up racism. He can't disavow the Klan and the Nazis and the whiteys because he loves them and needs them.

Racism is his secret sauce.

It's what sets him apart from his fellow Republicans - the willingness to say blatantly racist things in public and not even try to pretend you're not racist. It's what brings those throngs of eager enthusiastic white people to his "rallies." It's what blew him past all those other Republicans in the primaries. It's what gave those thousand white boy nitwits the courage to drop their masks and pick up tiki torches and invade Charlottesville. It's what 34 percent of Americans (and 74 percent of Republicans) still like about him.

We can get rid of Trump, but he's just their leader.

Sep 2, 2017, 5:15 PM

Breaking: Joel Osteen will contribute $40m to a project attempting to fit a camel through the eye of a needle.

Sep 5, 2017, 11:34 PM

Cruelty is the only thing he's good at.

Sep 11, 2017, 6:41 AM

Sixteen years ago today, I was sitting at my desk in the East Village of Manhattan when the first of four hijacked passenger jets was turned into a missile. After that, you were for us or against us. We went to war with terror, a concept, and failed to defeat it. We spent our young soldiers' lives on the deserts of Iraq for no reason, for a mirage of WMD. We killed bin Laden but it didn't give us anything more than a momentary satisfaction. We struggled along in Iraq and Afghanistan, as the terrorists had surely intended.

We raised up a new tower, and made a gigantic, overscaled memorial to a tragedy that is even now fading into a memory with no clear meaning.

Our country came together for a moment, then fell apart in ways that are only becoming clear today.

Sep 22, 2017, 5:06 AM

Which fact do you think would drive Ho Chi Minh the most crazy?

1/ A new luxury condo tower in Ha Noi named for Louis XIV, "the Sun King." In the country where the French were defeated at Dien Bien Phu. In the capital of "Socialist Viet Nam."

2/ The two dominant fast-food players at Ha Noi's fancy new international airport terminal are Burger King and Popeye's Chicken.

3/ The United States gives billions in aid every year to Saudi Arabia, which sent the hijackers to destroy the World Trade Center, but never paid a single cent in reparations to Viet Nam after 20 years of unprovoked war and terror.

Oct 13, 2017, 1:02 PM

He is for nothing. He is against everything. He lives to negate, bloviate, frustrate, masturbate, obfuscate, denigrate. The only person he loves is his daughter. No one loves him, especially his daughter.

Oct 30, 2017, 8:08 AM

Any day Trump's campaign manager surrenders to the FBI is a yellow dog Democratic holiday. I'm celebrating with a bucket of KFC, two scoops of ice cream and a double covfefe on the rocks. May he be the first of many.

Oct 31, 2017, 8:07 PM

My brother Alan took me to the Saints game Sunday in New Orleans. As we were entering our section of the Superdome, "The Star-Spangled Banner" began to play. The large policeman at the entrance to our section refused to let us pass, forced us to stand there, and stand still, until the song was finished playing.

I respect my country but I do not enjoy being forced by armed policemen to demonstrate that respect. If my brother hadn't been with me, I'd probably have taken a knee. And gone to jail or at least gotten some boos. But I was a coward, a true chickenshit. I went along, I stood still until they finished playing the song.

America has changed. In small ways. By degrees. The death of liberty by a thousand cuts. And when we give in, as I did, we help them do it to us.

Nov 10, 2017, 2:17 AM

ROY MOORE: Hell she told me she was 15
AIDE: Age of consent was 16
ROY: Maybe she said 14
AIDE: 16 would be better
ROY: She looked about 12, to be honest
AIDE: OK this is not helping

Nov 10, 2017, 6:48 PM

1. Pro-pedophilia Republicans, please stand over there to the right and form a quiet line. Thank you.

2. Anti-pedophilia Republicans, please stand to the left and refrain from catcalls. Thank you.

3. Republicans undecided on pedophilia, please stand in the middle and await your turn. Thank you.

4. Children, young people anyone under 18 - please come form a line over here behind me. Refrain from talking to the people in groups 1-3. Thank you.

Nov 11, 2017, 5:57 AM

Trump says he asked Putin if Putin meddled in our election, and Putin says Oh heck no, Dude, why would you even SAY that, plus Trump says he seemed a bit PO'd even being asked about it again, and also, Vladimir's shoulders are so strong and broad, and he wears this XO body spray that is so arousing, it makes Donald feel faint. Like he is young again holding a bowling trophy. And OMG they wore the same shirt! And Donald will never EVER wash that shirt because... just because.

Nov 24, 2017, 9:06 PM

When Time chooses "Man of the Year"
One option seems perfectly clear
I'll put my own hint in:
Name Hillary Clinton,
Sit back, and await the Bronx cheer

Nov 27, 2017 9:34 PM

I moved to Ha Noi almost exactly two years ago. Everyone always asks why, and all I can I say is, you have to come to Ha Noi to understand. It's a place that makes you fall in love with it. Also, Papa was a rolling stone, and I take after him. I'm walking to New Orleans now, and I'll be stateside in 2018. But I'll always come back to Viet Nam. Until then, Tam biet and love to all my dear ones in Ha Noi.....

Dec 2, 2017, 8:53 AM
[Jim Nabors, 87, TV's Gomer Pyle, Is Dead]

When I was a boy I loved Jim Nabors because I sensed there was something soft and sweet in him that had nothing to do with being a Marine. Dad liked him because they were both from Sylacauga, Ala., and went to the same school a couple years apart. "He was just a regular kid," my Dad said.

There was something about Gomer that was like me - he liked girls, especially Lou Anne Poovy, but even more he seemed to enjoy spending time with his fellow Marines in his quonset hut.

After "Pyle," Jim Nabors had a quieter but more satisfying career. He met a Honolulu fireman and they lived together for 38 years. In 2013 they were finally able to get married. It was no big deal, Nabors assured his fans, but nice to "finally have rights as a couple."

I met Jim and Stan for lunch shortly after their marriage. I saw how well Stan took care of Jim, and I was able to thank Jim for being a role model to another gay Alabama kid. He was a real hero to me. The first openly gay celebrity from the state of Alabama. He led the way. Golllaaaay, shazayum, and good night.

Dec 8, 2017, 9:29 AM

The famous metafictional novelist William Gass died this week. In a collision of odd circumstance I appeared on two panels with him at a literary conference in Cologne, Germany, in 1995. He was a friendly, blunt, sarcastic man. Near the end of our first panel, Gass offered the opinion that novelists like myself who deal mostly in realistic fiction are corrupt water-carriers for the traditional literature machine and should be banished from the earth. I was so astonished that he had chosen me as the example of everything wrong with today's novelist that I sat more or less speechless for the rest of the panel.

That night I sat up late in my German hotel, making notes, scribbling furious defenses of writers like Mailer and John Gardner and Joan Didion who used the stuff of real life and were just as worthy as some existentialist experiment in metafictional omni-points of view. I got my argument all honed and ready. (Had to do it without the internet, too - this was 1995.)

At the panel the next day, I sallied forth with a summary of Gass' comments the day before. I delivered my opening soliloquy in defense of realistic fiction. He looked upon me with amusement and a bit of a twinkle. He then announced that I had invented the whole thing, he'd said nothing of the kind, he loved many realistic novelists and meant to celebrate them now, in this panel.

The audience smiled at me and my presumption. Only I and the few people who'd also been at yesterday's panel realized how master-fully I'd been set up.

Later we drank some of that light sweet lager they have in Cologne, and Gass told me he had never enjoyed a literary conference more. I told him I had.

Dec 12, 2017, 4:59 PM

This may look silly in a couple of hours, but I am putting a bet on the good Democratic voters of Alabama being more motivated than other Alabamians today. If the votes are fairly counted, I think Doug Jones will pull off a squeaker. *[He did.]*

Dec 15, 2017, 2:48 PM

Ah, New York! It started snowing five minutes after our plane landed. Then a woman screamed at me on the LaGuardia bus at length for no reason. Everyone shrank from me as if I were a virus-carrier.

The bus driver looked at me in the rear view and said, "What do you want me to do?" I shrugged.

The woman said "I am off my meds so don't fuck with me!" She murmured into her phone for awhile then got off the bus.

As soon as she was gone, everyone on the bus became my instant friend. They offered me seats, smiles. As I got off at 125th Street the driver said, Not everybody in New York like that. I said Yeah, I know.

2018

Jan 4, 2018, 7:55 PM

Shouldn't we be able to sue politicians for malpractice? One president can hurt a lot more people than a stadium full of bad doctors.

Jan 6, 2018, 9:05 AM

"I can handle things. I'm smart. Not like everybody says, like dumb. I'm smart and I want respect!" - Fredo Corleone

We've never had a president who told us he was smart. We had one who told us he was not a crook. I didn't believe him either.

Donald J. Trump ✔
@realDonaldTrump

....to President of the United States (on my first try). I think that would qualify as not smart, but genius....and a very stable genius at that!

6:30 AM · Jan 6, 2018   ⓘ

♡ 118.2K   ♡ 118.7K people are Tweeting about this

Jan 7, 2018, 9:49 PM

Now that I'm a very stable genius
I must take care to say what I meanius
If I twitter it wrong
I can hear them all yawn
And they'll see how unstable I've beenius.

Jan 11, 2018, 3:23 PM

In sixth grade I was a real smartass. I remember Mr. Wagner calling me down in class with the words, "Don't be facetious, young man." I was dying inside because I didn't know what facetious meant.

I waited all morning, until on the way to recess I dropped by the huge dictionary on its blond wood pedestal beside the door.

Mr. Wagner came back in and caught me at it. "Looking up facetious?" he said.

"Yes sir."

"What does it mean?" he said.

"Treating a serious subject with deliberately inappropriate humor,'" I read.

"Did I use the word appropriately?"

"Yes sir," I said.

I pretended to be regretful, but once I learned what it meant, I became facetious full-time.

Jan 13, 2018, 7:47 AM

Friday: Trump drops a leak about paying hush money to a pornstar, to distract from

Thursday: Trump says Haiti and all of Africa are "shithole countries," to distract from

Wed, Tues: blue wave for "President Oprah," which was in reaction to

Mon, Sun, Sat: Wolff book reveals Bannon says Trump is batshit, Trumps are traitors, which distracted from....

See a pattern?

Jan 13, 2018, 4:50 PM

Trump hasn't commented on the Hawaii missile scare because he's still trying to reach the President of Hawaii. Patience, people!

Jan 14, 2018, 3:45 PM

Yes it is possible even in 2018 for a nuclear war to begin because somebody clicked the wrong button on a mouse in Hawaii and somebody else was golfing in Florida and somebody in Pyongyang maybe didn't get the memo and whatever somebody tweeted latest is either an overture or a declaration of war, depending on how much cocaine someone has had this morning, but at least we have the reassurance of knowing we can rely on the steady hand and good commonsense of Kim Jung Un to keep his hand off the nuclear button.

Jan 19, 2018, 11:25 PM

What could be more appropriate than a government shutdown to mark his first year in office?

Jan 21, 2018, 12:25 PM

If a million people had taken to the streets in cities nationwide to protest the first year of Barack Obama's presidency, the major media would have given it more than 10 seconds at the end of "Nightly News."

If a million *white* MEN actually got it together to march to protest anything, they'd be giving it round-the-clock coverage. As they did every time a few dozen white men waved Confederate flags and called themselves the Tea Party in 2009.

Jan 30, 2018, 8:31 AM

Here is why the State of our Union is so unbelievably great.

1. Rich people who own stocks are 27 percent richer.
2. White people who don't like black and brown or foreign people or women, or just think life would be better if we didn't have to look at or hear from so many of them, are 78 percent more likely to reveal their bigotry on social media.
3. The point of view of white, angry, uneducated people has never been so fully explored by the New York Times. Take that, educated elite!
4. "Today the president* attacked X" has become the standard opening phrase on the evening news.
5. Porn actresses are getting, and giving, more jobs.

6. The president* has not acted on his sexual attraction to his daughter, as far as we know.

7. Rachel Maddow is the #1 ratings star of cable news.

8. "Celebrity Apprentice" is off the air

9. Generations of families are being ripped apart and deported in order to reduce the prevalence of taco trucks

10. Migratory birds will soon be eliminated, keeping our swamps and parks much cleaner

11. Mt. Karma is a high peak when you climb up the back side, but eventually you reach the top and there's nowhere but down.

Jan 30, 2018, 6:27 PM

Things I will be doing tonight to make sure I don't accidentally watch the State of the Union speech:

1. Sticking long needles in each eye
2. Hurling self over freeway guardrail
3. Detonating high explosives near each eardrum

Jan 31, 2018, 6:55 AM

I liked the part in his speech where he said we were all Americans, and that all Americans were once immigrants – except for the Native Americans, upon whom we committed genocide because we found they didn't make good slaves, so we kidnapped half the continent of Africa and brought them here in chains, then fought a war trying to keep them in chains, then "freed" them only to deny them everything, and re-enslaved them with Jim Crow. We spent a whole century keeping them down, saw the light in the 1960s and began making progress, and even elected a brilliant and effective African-American man as president – then in reaction we elected, with the help of our most powerful adversary Russia, a white supremacist who hates all immigrants, legal and non, and who is the most openly racist President ever to occupy the Oval Office.

The state of the Union is: dirty. in need of a good housecleaning.

Feb 1, 2018, 5:40 PM

Let's pity poor Hope, Stormy, Nikki,
One thing they have in common: icky.
Ambition is one thing,
I know it's the done thing,
But fighting o'er that little dicky?

Donald J. Trump ✔ @realDonaldTrump · 1h

This memo totally vindicates "Trump" in probe. But the Russian Witch Hunt goes
on and on. Their was no Collusion and there was no Obstruction (the word now
used because, after one year of looking endlessly and finding NOTHING,
collusion is dead). This is an American disgrace!

💬 31K   ↻ 14K   ♡ 47K   ✉

Mark Childress
@markchildress

Replying to @realDonaldTrump

I love that you put "Trump" in quotes. I think
I'll start doing that, "Trump." Get out of the
White House, "Trump." Resign, "Trump." I
really like this! Thanks, "@realDonaldTrump!"

10:57 AM - 3 Feb 2018

💬   ↻   ♡   ili

Feb 16, 2018, 4:35 PM

Trump's evening ahead:

- Cybersecurity meeting with Barron
- Phone call w/ VP (Moscow time)
- Hush money panel meets, ceremonial check signing
- Burnt steak
- 2 scoops
- The clik, clik, clik of angry heels in the hall, up and down, up and
down

Feb 23, 2018, 7:24 AM
[After the mass shooting at Parkland High School in Florida]

To the tune of "School Days"

Hardened Target Days, Hardened Target Days
'Hide your face in the carpet' days
Readin' and writin' and 'rithmetic
Who is the kid with the killing stick?
We had an active shooter drill
Teacher shot Jim, and Ann, and Bill
And I wrote on my phone, "I love you still"
When we were a couple of kids

Feb 28, 2018, 8:01 AM

After learning that Barbra Streisand has cloned her favorite terrier twice, I have written to Barack Obama asking for a hair sample.

Mar 3, 2018, 6:14 PM

The New York Times has done its 435th story on how Trump is depressed, angry, lashing out at friend and foe.

I haven't seen one New York Times story on how Trump has made the majority of us feel! You know, the majority of us who voted for Hillary Clinton. We exist too! We have needs! And feelings! We are snowflakes in search of a shovel!

Mar 7, 2018, 6:05 PM

Traditional marriage should only be between one man, his third wife, and a pornstar. Doesn't matter if one is a KGB agent. These are God's laws.

Mar 12, 2018, 9:39 PM

I have finally solved the gun problem in America: from now on, people must be required by law to have bulletproof children.

Mar 13, 2018, 8:42 PM

It must be hard to be Rex Tillerson today. You were massively powerful, King of Exxon, rich, admired, headed for golden retirement. Now you've been humiliated and fired by your boss, whom you called a "fucking moron." And he fired you in a TWEET.

Mar 14, 2018, 12:20 AM

Stephen Hawking could no longer bear to live in this particular universe, and has gone off in search of someplace better.

There are at least 7 billion alternate universes in which Stephen Hawking is now busting a move like Michael Jackson.

(Too soon for a Hawking joke? Yes. It is also too late, and it is happening at the same time as itself, and in two places at once.)

Mar 19, 2018, 7:54 AM

Trump's schedule for today:

* Fox&Friends briefing via teleconference (President's Lav)

* Executive Time

* Tweet consultation with @KellyAnnePolls

* Float trial balloon: massive assault on Democrat moon while it is in full-moon stage and easier to hit

* Eat a baby

* Executive Time

*. Fire three most-loyal employees, strip most loyal of pension

* Stormy (phone)

* 18 holes

* Enter Mar-A-Lago Simulation Chamber for party rehearsal

* Find a cute puppy and kill slowly with hands. Kelly will eat

* Blast Betty White as "nincompoop white-head"

* Masturbate frequently but to no avail

* Melania verbal abuse 15 mins per contract

* Melania's verbal abuse of POTUS 15 mins per contract

* Steak, burnt, two scoops

* Snif

Apr 1, 2018, 7:34 AM
If Easter always fell on April Fool's Day, Jesus would be known as the greatest practical joker of all time.

Apr 4, 2018, 8:02 AM
On a sticky Thursday in April, forty years ago today, I heard on the radio that Bobby Kennedy was going to make a campaign stop that very afternoon at the Muncie airport. Bobby had been my hero since they shot his brother in Dallas. He was handsome and often played touch football with his kids in the pages of Life. I dreamed that he was my Dad. I was thrilled when he decided to run for President. I believed he deserved to win, especially after they shot his brother in the head.

I raced from school to Mrs. Anders' house for our Cub Scout meeting. Within five minutes I had convinced her to drive our Scout Den out to the Muncie airport to watch Bobby Kennedy's plane land. It was an easy sell, because as it turned out Mrs. Anders had a thing for Bobby, too. "What a great experience for you boys to see our next President," she said. "Plus we can count it towards our Citizenship badge. What a great suggestion, Mark!"

I beamed. So proud of myself. Brian Anders stuck out his tongue at me.

When the other boys arrived we piled into Mrs. Anders' brown station wagon. The other boys had only a vague idea who Bobby Kennedy was, but they were happy enough for us to skip the stick-whittling and oath-reciting and go forth on an actual adventure.

At once they all set up a racket for milkshakes. At once Mrs. Anders gave in, which was her duty as a good Den Mother. We wasted the next thirty minutes at John's Awful-Awful Hamburgers ("Awful Awful Good!") while the clock ticked slower every minute. By the time we got back in the car I was near frantic with worry that Bobby Kennedy would have already landed and gone.

That part of Indiana was so flat he could have set his airplane down most anywhere. The Muncie airport offered a squat little terminal building, a windsock on a striped pole, a runway surrounded by a chain-link fence. A couple hundred people milled and chatted in front of a gap in the fence, waiting for Bobby Kennedy.

Mrs. Anders spied a couple of her friends. She warned us to stay within sight, and let us run.

We ran around in that crowd for two hours, though it seemed much longer because we didn't know how long it would be. Some older boys organized a hundred-yard-dash competition across one end of the parking lot. We raced until we were out of breath, with white stars whizzing past our eyes. At last a large airplane swooped down over the field, a loud shiny-silver four-propeller job. The tires chirped touching the runway. The plane trundled over the tarmac toward us, revving its engines and blowing up dust.

All at once the loose easygoing crowd turned into a mob, tripping and pushing each other in the rush to the fence.

Over their heads I saw a stairway roll up to the side of the plane. A burst of photo flashes as a waving man appeared – was it him? I couldn't tell. The crowd swirled around me and pushed me back.

I lost sight of Mrs. Anders and the other Cub Scouts. It was scary in there among the knees of the struggling, shoving grownups, oddly quiet but for the scrabble of shoe leather on pavement. Everyone was trying to get close to him. Nobody was making any other kind of sound.

I remembered on TV how the girls screamed as they trampled each other trying to touch a Beatle. This was quiet – like being lost in the cornfield behind our house – I could see no more than a few feet in any direction.

A hum arose from the jostling knot of humanity passing a few feet in front of me. TV lights nodded in and out of view.

I took a deep breath and cried, "We love you, Bobby!"

My voice came out high and pipey, a real boy soprano. In the muffled silence of the crowd, it came out a lot louder than I intended.

That whole part of the crowd laughed at me.

The blood in my face heated up.

I sensed a churning movement among the jostling, a change of direction, elbows and knees growing denser then suddenly opening up to a brilliant light.

Outlined in the haze of artificial light, a man bent down with his hand outstretched to me. His shock of hair was brighter and grayer than on TV. Behind him, a smiling lady – a miniskirt, long white--stockinged legs, upswept hairdo, Bugs Bunny teeth –

Bobby Kennedy's hand closed on mine. Soft, surprisingly warm. A dry current of electricity lanced through my arm, tingling my shoulder. "Nice to see you, son," he said. Shook my hand, clapped me on the shoulder and was swallowed in an instant by the crowd.

The lights bowed and nodded away.

Nice to see you, son. I imagine that he is my Dad, all these people will vanish and we will play touch football while a Life photographer snaps handsome black-and-white photos of us.

Bobby's entourage piled into a line of black Fords. The word motorcade swam up in my mind with its deadly aroma of Dallas. I saw no convertibles in this motorcade.

In a rush I realized where I'd seen the toothy woman – in the pages of Life. Short skirt and white-frosted legs, coming out of a church. That was Ethel! His wife!

For some reason, seeing Ethel made it a hundred times more real. I stood flash-frozen to the spot where it happened. I couldn't move. I couldn't believe it had happened, but that was Ethel Kennedy and so it must be true.

Bobby Kennedy shook my hand and spoke to me.

Mrs. Anders found me standing there, thunderstruck. "Well, did you see him?" she said. "I couldn't get within twenty feet of him!"

I told her the whole thing. How he was about to pass by, but I cried out so he stopped, turned around and came back through that crowd to find me.

I'm not sure she believed me entirely.

My face still burned from the moment after I said "Bobby, we love you" too loud. I felt as if Jesus had touched me, or the Beatles, someone absolutely important and immortal in a history-of-the-world kind of way.

Bobby's magical Kennedy energy rushed down my arm and left the whole right side of my body sore and throbbing, tingling all the way home.

I bounded across our sidewalk in exaggerated leaps like a crazed ballet dancer. I turned cartwheels on our front yard.

I ran into the house, to the back bathroom, to examine myself in the full-length mirror. I was sure I would find myself transformed: my arm swollen, or hanging differently than my other arm . . . some kind of special new light in my eyes. Something to signify the change.

. . . Nothing. I was the same.

Except that my arm was now the secret center of the universe. Bobby Kennedy touched it and made it special – not just my hand. My whole arm.

The next day I realized with a shiver that it was possible Bobby was shaking my hand at the exact moment they shot Martin Luther King in Memphis. The fact that I happened to be shaking his hand at about the time the shots rang out seemed to me strange and dangerous, far too important to share with anyone.

Bobby flew on to Indianapolis that night. He went to a rough neighborhood, climbed up on the back of a truck, and made a famous speech about forgiveness.

It didn't matter. The cities burned anyway. But not Indianapolis, so that was something anyway.

For a couple of months I felt important. The lightning-bolt of history had passed through my hand. I did not tell anyone because I knew they would laugh at me, as the crowd had laughed when I called Bobby's name.

Then another lightning bolt struck, in a pantry of the Ambassador Hotel in Los Angeles. My first thought when I heard he was dead: It's my fault.

If I hadn't convinced Mrs. Anders to take us to the Muncie airport that day – if I hadn't got lost in that forest of grownups and called out to Bobby – if I hadn't made him turn around and come back to shake my hand – wouldn't his life have kept moving along the same track, one minute earlier? Wouldn't he have passed through that hotel pantry a full minute before Sirhan Sirhan got into firing position?

Maybe it was just my eagerness to imagine the universe revolving around me. But no one could deny I was one tiny event in the hectic crush of Bobby Kennedy's life that led him to that pantry and six firecrackers pop! pop! pop! pop! pop! pop!

Apr 5, 2018, 6:44 PM

A helpful rule of thumb: if you don't believe everything Donald Trump says, you're not the one he's talking to.

Apr 13, 2018, 5:01 PM

Normalization 101: When the New York Times refers unironically to the president's fixer without putting quotes around it.

Presidents don't have fixers. Mob bosses have fixers. The Times drops that word casually, as if all heads of state have "fixers."

Apr 16, 2018, 10:22 AM

Waiter's Favorite Question: "Are you still working on that?"

"Yes, like the cavemen of yore, whose entire lives consisted of tracking and slaying the animal that would sustain them through another brutal week, I am still *working* on this! Thank you!"

Apr 20, 2018, 7:06 AM

Kay Ivey, governor of Alabama, says that Alabama doesn't need "out of state liberals" telling Alabamians how to behave.

If it weren't for those well-known out-of-state liberals Lincoln and Ulysses S Grant, of course, she'd be riding in a carriage in a hoopskirt and her slave would be driving.

People from Alabama either love Trump or loathe him, but mostly we are not surprised by him, because we grew up with the example of George Corley Wallace. The banty rooster from Clio was Trump before Trump was Trump. He was America's most gifted popularizer of racism until the present day. But Corley was smart and had a real gift for gab, as when he made fun of "pointy-head college professors who can't even park a bicycle straight... "

When I was a young reporter I was assigned to cover his supposed "farewell concert" at the coliseum in Montgomery. Tammy Wynette sang "Stand By Your Man" to the marginally sentient man in the wheelchair. I went back to the newsroom in Birmingham and wrote a goodbye-forever piece for the News that was probably kinder than it should have been.

Four years later, damned if the old bastard didn't come back to life and win another whole term.

Apr 21, 2018, 1:03 PM

Melania: What it means in tweet, this "flip?"
Donald: Don't worry about it.
M. No, tell me. In tweet you says people is to "flip" if government is mean. Like getting out of some troubles?
D. I tell you, it's just legal mumbo-jumbo. Do you want some new shoes? Go buy some shoes. Whatever you want.
M. So if somebody is "flip," means they telling government all bad things they can knowing about you?
D. That's not what it means. Look, if your English was better -
M. Shut up! My English be getting more best every day.
D. Yes it is.
M. So if you wants somebody not "flip," how much you pay?

D. It depends. Look I've got to get ready for golf.
M. When you finish from golf, I being right here. (smiles)

Apr 28, 2018, 7:46 AM

"Have you had enough? No? Well, more me
Is fine with the ones who adore me
As long as I pillory
Obama and Hillary
Fake Christians don't even mind Stormy"

11:58 AM

If the pace of my speech seems excessive
And my temper a little aggressive,
One thing you must admit
(And the shoe seems to fit) -
For a moron, I'm very impressive

12:29 PM

It's hard to make love to Melania
When you've also had porn stars upon ya
A goodbye would be nice
Au revoir would suffice
But in Russian they say *"do svidaniya"*

May 3, 2018, 4:47 PM

To the tune of "My Favorite Things," apologies to Richard Rodgers.

Wiretaps on Cohen, denials from Rudy,
Mueller's amused, you can bet your patootie,
Secret indictments all tied up with string
These are a few of my favorite things

Sarah's offended, Ms. Conway's insulted
Even Steve Bannon has now been consulted
What song is Manafort planning to sing?
What will he tell of my favorite things?

Poor Dr. Ronny will give no more candy
Crazy Doc Bornstein sure did come in handy
Viagra, Propecia, a few pornstar flings,
I got the shots for a lot of those things

Crisp bills, one hundreds, nonsequential numbers,
Plots that sound like a brand-new "Dumb and Dumber,"
Investigations don't happen to kings
This is not one of my favorite things

When my hair falls
When the wife bites
When I'm feeling Sad
I simply get rid of a few underlings
And then I don't feel so bad!

May 8, 2018, 2:52 PM
    Okay I'm hearing there has been a lot of criticism about the odd name of Melania's new project, "Be Best." So the White House has decided to change it to "Be You're Best."

May 9, 2018, 3:15 PM

Because Donald Trump lacks a long wang,
And has run out of porn stars to bang,
He'll sell out South Korea
And soon you will see a
Brand-new Trump Hotel in Pyongyang

May 11, 2018, 7:39 AM

Melania seethes in her pink bedroom. "Where can be MY secret slush fund for wife? Why only pornstar and Playboy girl have slush fund? No slush fund for WIFE? How can BE BEST without slush fund?"

May 19, 2018, 10:19 AM

Dear Princess Markle, Be as nice as possible to your husband's grandmother. On this date in 1536 Anne Boleyn lost her head in the Tower of London, just sayin, best wishes.

May 23, 2018, 6:04 PM

Selfishly, of course, I am appalled by the federal judge's ruling that Trump cannot block people on Twitter, because as you know being blocked by Trump is one of my fondest dreams. I was just going to scratch that one off my life list and invent my own Trump nickname for myself: Stupid Mark! Failing Mark! Stupid Failing Mark is a one man Witch Hunt!

Then I realized Trump will never obey this ruling. And Twitter won't force him to.

May 30, 2018, 12:11 AM

Is it racist of me to pine for another Black President? Probably. But I think it is the surest way toward healing America - one fine Black President after another until we break the back of racism for good.

May 30, 2018, 9:18 PM

I was riding my bike in the bike lane yesterday when a visitor from Florida opened his car door into me. Bam crash pow! Broke my left wrist and arm DANG OW it hurts so my entries will be one-handed, brutish, and short for the time being.

Florida Man got mad and yelled at me because my arm dented his door!

Jun 1, 2018, 10:17 AM

Trump didn't go to Texas to visit the grieving families of the Santa Fe school shooting. He went to attend a $5000-a-plate fundraiser. And made the families meet him at the airport.

Jun 6, 2018, 9:39 AM

I will always remember this day – the first time I heard that the United States of America is separating immigrant children from their families and keeping them in cages.

Jun 11, 2018, 7:53 AM

Trump: Give up your nukes and I'll give you anything you want
Kim: I strapped my uncle to a cannon and blew him to pieces and had it filmed in super slow-mo
Trump: What about a McDonald's? Right there in downtown Pyongyang

Jun 11, 2018, 9:24 AM

Kim: I will leave Singapore today at 2
Trump: I will leave Singapore two hours before Kim leaves
K: I already left Singapore
T: I have never even been to Singapore
K: There is no Singapore
T: I hereby declare war on Canada

Jun 13, 2018, 8:23 AM

When meeting with dictators, I
Like to look the guy straight in the eye,
His wish, my command
How nice, shaking his hand
And we both got two scoops with our pie

Jun 15, 2018, 1:39 PM

No matter how deluded and inflated Trump is, the news of Manafort's jailing had to have rung a tiny bell inside his head - "could that be me?"

Jun 15, 2018, 7:45 AM

Trump on Kim Jong Un on Fox & Friends: "He speaks and his people sit up in attention. I want my people to do the same."

Jun 16, 2018, 6:54 AM

The summer of 1970 I was twelve going on thirteen and I wanted so badly to be cool. Cool was all over the TV. Cool was Steve McQueen and Napoleon Solo and the man from U.N.C.L.E. Everybody in the world was cool but me. Everybody had bell-bottom pants except me. I begged my grandmother, and she made me a pair. They were white. The bells were red and blue wide stripes. They must have been astonishingly ridiculous to see. Luckily nobody took a picture. I wore those bell-bottoms everywhere that summer. I wore them to the drive-in to see "Butch Cassidy and the Sundance Kid." It was rated M, for Mature audiences only. It was very racy. I was so goddamn cool in my bell-bottoms.

Jun 23, 2018, 12:45 AM

Let me just pause a moment to reflect that the minority (ruling) party of this country is trying hard to convince you that baby concentration camps are a good idea.

This is the policy of an inhuman person who believes his opponents are weak people who will cave in to him to save the wailing children. The cries of the children are music to his ears.

Jun 22, 2018, 9:44 AM

Is it rude to point out that Melanie's "I Really Don't Care Do U" jacket is the most honest member of the Trump administration to date? Also, "I Really Don't Care, Do U?" is an anagram of "Neurotically Adored."

Jun 24, 2018, 8:23 AM

I'm conflicted about Sarah Sanders being asked to leave the Red Hen restaurant because the owner hates Trump. My first reaction was that the restaurateur, plainly a woman of conscience, had handed Sanders a cudgel with which to beat the left for our supposed "intolerance."

The everyday American is now angrier than the politicians who are supposed to represent us. We can no longer sit in silence and watch fascists take over our country.

It's not just a technicality that Sanders was not asked to leave because she was the wrong race, color, religion, sexual orientation, or national origin. She was barred as an individual the way you would bar O.J. Simpson if he came to your restaurant and you didn't want to serve a murderer. The proprietor has every right to bar people she thinks are criminals from her place of business.

Maybe...if our Dem leaders (Mr. Obama, where are you? Mr. Biden? I can't hear you) are going to continue their dignified silence, we the citizens have to fight them ourselves, one farm-to-table restaurant at a time.

Jun 27, 2018, 8:04 AM

Republicans like to justify their bad acts by claiming Obama did it first, which is odd since they also claim Obama was the worst President ever. "It's OK because the worst president did it first" is kinda nutso, if you ask me which nobody did.

Jul 2, 2018, 7:35 AM

Millions of Americans in more than 700 cities hit the streets Saturday amid a summer heat wave to protest Trump's cruel, anti-American immigration policies. But if you look at the front page of Sunday's New York Times and Washington Post, you wouldn't know a thing about it.

I remember both papers' generous coverage of the hundreds or dozens of Tea Party protesters in 2010. Now that millions are taking to the streets, it isn't news. Let four Trumpy segregationists gather in a diner in Pennsylvania to laud their hero, and believe me the Times and the Post will be there!

Jul 3, 2018, 3:46 PM

Why is everybody so concerned with Trump wanting to meet Putin one-on-one with no note takers or official record? Haven't you ever had a boyfriend you haven't seen for a long time? Did you want a bunch of witnesses around for your first reunion? No, I didn't think you did!

Jul 4, 2018, 7:49 PM

Dearest Mother, Our battalion is down to one box of Tic Tacs and a can of biscuits that are not gluten-free. Gen. Coulter's army was smashed upon the field at Bowling Green but bitter remnants fight on savagely. Our exhaustion is profound. Please send Starbucks gift cards - all you have - yr obt svt Kyle

Jul 5, 2018, 7:34 AM

The lady who paid to shoot the rare giraffe will appear on the "Today Show" tomorrow "to explain her side of the story." The giraffe is unavailable for comment.

Jul 9, 2018, 7:57 PM

   With the news that Trumpy will nominate Brett Kavanaugh to the Supreme Court, just a reminder to set your clocks back 50 years tonight.

Jul 10, 2018, 7:10 AM

FutureTranscript™

TRUMP: I won by the biggest margin ever, biggest crowds ever
QE2:
TRUMP: Hey Queen, ever think about turning this dump into a hotel?
QE2:
TRUMP: Somebody get these dogs outa here? Chrissake.
QE2:
TRUMP: So I really liked that one chick - Diana? She was HOT. Did you know her?
QE2:
TRUMP: You people call this a hamburger?

Jul 10, 2018, 12:54 PM

FutureTranscript™

TRUMP: Everybody is saying I'd be a better queen than you, cause I'd be a king
QE2:
TRUMP: Have you seen my daughter? I might be dating her.
QE2:
TRUMP: Only an idiot would drive on the wrong side of the road, am I right?
QE2:
TRUMP: Did you ever get to meet Abe Lincoln?

Jul 10, 2018, 6:30 PM

FutureTranscript™

TRUMP: A bunch of your grandparents got their heads chopped off

QE2:

TRUMP: Did you ever get to meet Hitler? Did he give you any presents?

QE2:

TRUMP: They said your sister was a hoot but that you were always kind of a stiff

QE2:

TRUMP: My inauguration crowds were bigger than the crowds for your funeral will be

QE2:

TRUMP: They said you were real chatty with Obama

QE2: Obama? What a *charming* man. And his wife, perfectly *lovely*.

TRUMP:

QE2: (drops mic)

Jul 11, 2018, 7:37 AM

FutureTranscript™

TRUMP: I heard you got a shitload of diamonds, so does my wife!

QE2:

TRUMP: I bet you hate Canada as much as me

QE2:

TRUMP: I own most of Scotland

QE2:

QE2:

QE2:

TRUMP: Well, I have a big golf course there.

QE2:

TRUMP: Didn't your mom have a colostomy bag made to look like a purse?

Jul 11, 2018, 9:36 AM

TRUMP: Did you see the map of my election, it was a sea of red with like these little blue places on it
QE2:
TRUMP: Are you even awake?
[Threatening corgi growl]
QE2:
TRUMP: Okay so I get that you speak English in England, where do you speak British
QE2:
TRUMP: Did you really have Princess Di knocked off? Because to me that whole thing looked totally fishy
QE2: [silently texting]
TRUMP: Who was your favorite Beatle

Jul 13, 2018, 7:01 AM

FutureTranscript™

Prince Philip: He's a bloody stinking idiot
QE2: Now Philip, we've met bloodier
PP: Oh really, love? Who?
QE2: Well, Benny Hill.
PP: An Einstein by comparison. Did you see the way he gnawed at that charred beefsteak? - swine
QE2: Mussolini without the charm
PP: I'll meet him but I won't shake his bloody hand
QE2: No telling where it's been. The wife is hilarious. Doesn't she look like Steven Tyler?
PP: ROFLMAO

Jul 15, 2018, 7:10 AM
[Trump prepares for a summit meeting with Vladimir Putin.]

The boy could barely sleep. Tomorrow was the day he'd been dreaming of for more than a year. He and his hero, alone in a room. Tomorrow he will show his hero how strong he is now. How big. How powerful in every way like his hero.

The boy crawled out of bed and looked in the mirror. His hair. The hair was not right. The hero would hate his hair. It was supposed to be flowy and swoopy. But now it was boxy. Square. Like a doughnut box on his head. The boy made a face at his reflection, and reached for his blow dryer.

Jul 16, 2018, 8:20 AM

FutureTranscript™

T: Everybody says I shouldn't meet with you alone because it looks like I'm working for you, ha ha
P:
T: Really bad, hacking our election like that, I know you hate Hillary but, you know, knock it off. Okay?
P:
T: I don't even know where Crimea is, but I know Ukraine girls are hot.
P:
T: You have to make it sound like I was really mean to you
P: I have tape of young Russian girls peeing on you
T:
P: I watch tape every day
T:
P: Ha just kidding
T: Well this has been a great meeting, just great

Jul 18, 2018, 8:22 PM

One person so terrified Vladimir Putin that he risked everything to target his clandestine forces to make sure she didn't get anywhere near the White House: Hillary Clinton.

Jul 20, 2018, 1:29 PM

Democrats are all, Just WAIT till Mueller proves he's a traitor who colluded with Russia and sold out the country! and Republicans are all, Look, unless he colluded with Hillary, we are not about to give even one fuck.

Jul 21, 2018, 6:57 AM

I keep hearing muttering about the coming "civil war."

Go to your local Wal-Mart and look at the people standing in the customer service line. These are their front-line troops. Walk back to the electronics department and watch five minutes of Fox News. Those are their generals, their leaders. Go to the pharmacy department - there's your cannon fodder, lined up with their walkers and mobility scooters, waiting for their prescriptions.

Jul 22, 2018 9:43 AM

Michael Cohen said he would take a bullet for Trump.

Trump said he could shoot somebody in the middle of Fifth Avenue.

Advice for Michael Cohen: avoid Fifth Avenue.

Jul 29, 2018, 3:35 PM

I'm just a ignorant ole country boy, but it seems pretty silly that we fight over energy and choke ourselves burning liquefied dinosaurs when we live on a ball of molten iron. Five to thirty kilometers below where you're sitting is all the energy we'll ever need. Then of course there's that vast ball of burning hydrogen in the sky.

Jul 30, 2018, 8:18 AM

Remember when the president wasn't like the mad dog loping down the street in 'To Kill a Mockingbird?' Although I felt sorry for that dog.

Aug 2, 2018, 9:45 PM

What do you miss the most about the days before the internet? Personally, I miss not having to care about peoples' cats. (I do, though. I care.)

Aug 2, 2018, 7:36 AM

"Woke up in a towering rage this morning, but my toadies have scheduled a rally for tonight. Rallies make me feel alive. They make my hands literally double in size. I give the fans my rage, and they give me their love. I drink in their love flowing across the footlights. I turn it into hate and spray it all over them and they love it.

"Tonight I shall improvise. I shall *jam*. I shall rattle world markets and destroy alliances. Vladimir will be proud of me. Daddy will love me in heaven. Daddy will know I am not just a loser with the hands of a baby. Not the dim bulb in the shandelear. NOT just a pisher from Queens."

Aug 2, 2018, 7:25 PM

Thinking how Ivanka's going to look after she comes out of prison and overcompensates with way too much plastic surgery.

Aug 3, 2018, 2:51 PM

Dear Diary,

I hate hate hate hate hate him! You know who! (Vladimir P.) We had a wonderful time in Helsinki, it was just like I dreamed it could be. He took me seriously, all my ideas! So as soon as I got home I begged Mother, please can I invite him over later in the year? After the summer term? PLEASE Mother, I begged, we had such a grand time in Helsinki, his family says yes, I know it can be pure magic if only he will come to Washington! Solid weeks of begging, finally she gave in.

So I said hey Vlad, wanna come to DC? You know what happened!!! He hemmed, he hawed, he said everything but YES. Finally something awkward about – No, I should come to Moscow first, meet his family. Like it's not important for him to meet MY family! I think it may be OVER. I really hate him! But do I still love him. Do I? Oh Diary, please tell me what to do?!?!?   – Confused in Love

Aug 4, 2018, 7:16 AM

LeBron James says Trump has been using sport "to divide us." Trump replies that LeBron James is stupid. He says Don Lemon is stupid. He says Maxine Waters is "low IQ." See a pattern? Not a "culture war," gatekeepers. It's presidential racism. Call it what it is.

Aug 4, 2018, 3:27 PM

Trump: "(Don Lemon) makes LeBron look smart, which isn't easy to do."

Aug 7, 2018, 8:50 AM

Please do not say "parm." You have plenty of time to say "Parmesan." I promise, you can spare the time it will take you to say the entire word. We are all happy to wait while you say it. Thank you very much.

Aug 9, 2018, 8:27 PM

Dearest Mother,

I have joined Space Force and we are off to attack the sun for president* Trump. The stupid Sun has insulted and burned innocent Earthlings for the last time! No more rising and setting at different times every day! We can do better. Remember Bowling Green!

White House
2:43 PM ET

ECLIPSE OF THE CENTURY
TRUMP WATCHES ECLIPSE FR(
Voice of Chad Myers | ams Meteorol

Aug 10, 2018, 5:47 PM

Dearest Mother,

We in the Space Force are weary. The Sun is much hotter than we had been led to believe. Our generals lied to us. They promised the Sun would be much cooler at night. Guess what. It's SUMMER! So it doesn't even matter.

HQ is considering an invasion of the Moon instead but no one is sure if we can find it in the dark.

Yr obdt son, Aloysius

Aug 11, 2018, 12:19 AM

Suicidal mechanic hijacks a Horizon Air Q400 from Seattle-Tacoma airport, flies it around Puget Sound, chased by a pair of F-15s, says he's going to disappoint a lot of people who loved him, then crashes the plane.

We've entered a new era in news. I learned the complete story of the hijack from Twitter, including crash of plane and taped bits of pilot's talk to the tower, before CNN broke into reruns with the first fragmentary live bulletin.

Aug 18, 2018, 8:34 AM

Kellyanne Conway: "Why is everybody so obsessed with the president of the United States that they can't even begin or finish a sentence without mentioning his name five times? It's kind of weird."

"Hindenburg" cocktail waitress: "Why is everybody so worried about that bright light outside the windows? The sun comes up every day."

Aug 20, 2018, 1:46 PM

If there's one thing Trump has taught us, it's that some of the people are remarkably stupid all of the time.

Aug 22, 2018, 7:51 PM

He used Russians to win an election
And pornstars to win an erection
His hands are so tiny
His face is his hiney
Like IMAX, he's good at projection

Aug 23, 2018, 9:45 AM

On May 29, Florida Man opened his car door into my bike on Camp Street and crashed me. Three months, seven broken bones, surgery, one titanium plate, seven screws, and eight weeks' physical therapy later, I am a happy boy today. I got to ride my bike for the first time!

Aug 23, 2018, 2:48 PM
[Trump splits publicly with David Pecker, owner of the "National Enquirer"]

Our president thinks he's a genius
When in fact he's a master of meanness
His friends all turn flips
While on twitter he quips
And continues to lead with his Pecker.

Aug 23, 2018, 7:02 PM
About the NFL kneeling protests. Can anybody name me any other protesting group who are told that what they're protesting is not what they're protesting?

Righties insist the NFL protests are not about police brutality, but are in fact about disrespecting the flag and the military.

Nobody told Martin Luther King his crusade was not about civil rights. At the very least, protesters have the right to define what they are protesting.

Aug 25, 2018, 10:16 AM
Working on a version of "The Christmas Song" for Trump to sing to Jeff Sessions. All I have so far is the first line: "Jeff's nuts roasting on an open fire..."

Aug 26, 2018, 7:48 PM
A happy thought! Maybe Trump will get so jealous of all the McCain memorial coverage that he'll go on and die out of spite.

For your consideration: The president* of the United States, putative leader of the republican party, publicly uninvited to the funeral of his own party's 2008 standard-bearer . . . and there's not one person in America who thinks that's a bad idea.

Aug 27, 2018, 7:42 AM

Trump ordered the flags at the White House raised back to full staff at midnight. He would rather see 24 hours of coverage of what an asshole he is than any more nice stuff about McCain.

Keep in mind: this is not just Trump being an asshole. It's a deliberate strategy to disrupt the news cycle and delight his base, which he has trained to despise anyone who will talk to a Democrat.

Aug 30, 2018, 8:03 PM

We're only supposed to speak kindly of the departed, and it is in the spirit of admiration and awe that I tell you of the time I ate dinner in a fancy NYC restaurant at the table beside the immortal Aretha Franklin's.

She was coming off one of her skinny spells. She ate dinner with three jolly guys. She ordered a roast chicken and ate the whole chicken herself. Then she ordered another roast chicken and ate that one too. Then she ordered chocolate cake for dessert. Aretha knew how to live!

Sep 9, 2018, 11:33 AM

What if George Stephanopoulos married George Papadopoulos and they had a son named Wop Bopaloobop Abopadopoulos?

Sep 9, 2018, 12:11 PM

To the tune of "The Beverly Hillbillies Theme"

Come a listen to a story bout a man named Don
Rich man from Queens, always felt so put upon
Then one day he was acting kinda crude
And up through the ground come his favorite food
Steak it was
Burnt steak
Ketchup glaze
Well the first thing you know ol' Don's the president*
Wife's folks said "Can you make me resident?"
Don said "Fine, if you sign an NDA"

And that's how they came to the good ol' USA
"The Slovenian Hillbillies" - brought to you by Kellogg's of Battle Creek

Sep 10, 2018, 7:49 AM

A man who can't pronounce "anonymous"
In high office, seems rather ominous.
We don't have to get all Deuteronomous:
Brains and power are rarely synonymous.

Sep 11, 2018, 9:11 PM

Wouldn't you think ONE Republican would want to go down in history as "the one who stopped Trump?" Just going on pure naked self-interest, I mean.

Sep 14, 2018, 1:26 PM

It's the most wonderful time of the year
With Bob Mueller plea-dealing
And Manafort squealing just like a pig's ear
It's the most wonderful time of the year!

It's the guilt-guiltiest season of all
With those Cyrillic greetings and Trump Tower meetings
When Reds come to call
It's the guilt-guiltiest season of all!

There'll be Junior in prison,
Ivanka's decision
To rat out the rest of her kin,
There'll be fake cover stories
And tales of the glories
Of all the votes he didn't win.....

It's the most wonderful time of the year!

There'll be lots of betrayals
And we'll hear the tales
Bob Woodward can't hear
It's the most wonderful time of the year!

Sep 15, 2018, 8:14 AM

Advisory: From Trump's point of view, nothing he says needs to be true, accurate, or even possible. It just has to be believable to the people who think he's a fine president. The next time he tells a bizarre lie, I must remember that. The unbelievability is the main point of what he says. He is constructing a fictional story, a fiction for his supporters to live in. They live in an angry editorial cartoon playing out in real time. The universe is out to get them, and he is their savior.

The story is not for our benefit. He doesn't care if we believe it or not. THEY BELIEVE. Reality is too much for them to face; they prefer his soothing story of white American male supremacy.

Sep 16, 2018, 4:34 PM

Next 4 days:

1. Kavanaugh accuser pilloried by right wing media until
2. Trump attacks her on twitter, while
3. Lindsey Graham turns charming pirouettes that
4. Give Grassley cover to proceed, so
5. Kavanaugh will be confirmed to the court for life Thursday
6. "Sorry, girls! Sucks to be you!"

Sep 17, 2018, 2:27 PM

Judge Kavanaugh denies he was at the party.

Dr. Ford says she doesn't remember the date of the party or exactly where it took place.

So how can he deny he was there?

Wouldn't his only truthful answer have to be "I can't possibly know if I was there without more information"?

As my dear old grandmother Stella used to say, "A hit dog will holler."

Sep 18, 2018, 3:43 PM
"Dear America, It didn't happen, it was "rough play" at a party I did not go to, in a place no one has yet named, with people whose names I did not know, on a date that has not been established. The reason I know it was "rough play" is because I was not there and did not ever do anything except the part I denied before, if that fits with what I said first."

Sep 19, 2018, 7:29 AM
"Why didn't she come forward sooner?" the Republicans cry, as death threats drive Dr. Christine Blasey Ford from her home and millions of Republicans take to the internet to destroy her.

Sep 28, 2018, 12:46 AM
A woman spoke her truth. A man shouted her down and the other men pronounced him the winner. They countered a charge of abusing women by abusing more women and then cheered themselves for it.

Oct 1, 2018, 12:19 PM
Kim and Trump are a fabulous new couple, far be it from me to wonder aloud if theirs is a love that will stand the test of time, or if Trump will start calling Kim too much too soon, & Kim will start turning off his phone, and Trump will send a series of increasingly desperate texts.

Oct 15, 2018, 6:52 PM
[News breaks of the murder of Jamal Khashoggi at the Saudi Embassy]
I will confess we got to the "covering up complicity in an actual murder" plotline rather earlier in this show than would normally be believable.

Oct 18, 2018, 7:10 AM

"Very fine people on both sides of that bone saw"
"Maybe it was a bone saw, maybe it was some 400-lb guy sitting on a bed"
"Looks like it was a runaway bone saw, a rogue, acting on its own"

Oct 23, 2018, 7:11 AM

Jared is such a delicate, bloodless little thing. Let's hope he never gets on the wrong side of his buddy, Crown Prince Bone Saw.

Oct 24, 2018 9:11 AM

Fog takes about 150 years off Orleans Avenue in the French Quarter.

Oct 24, 2018, 10:50 AM

"Somebody" sent pipe bombs to Obama, the Clintons, George Soros, Debbie Wasserman-Schultz. Maybe more. Somebody.

Might want to check the smoke detectors in the Reichstag.

Oct 25, 2018, 8:52 PM

Felix's Oyster Bar has been on Iberville Street since 1885. The heyday was probably in the 1940s when Carlos Marcello was the owner and you could place your horse bets or play your numbers with your raw dozen. One of Marcello's bookies was "Dutz" Morret, a local lowlife who leaned on Marcello to get a job here for his loser nephew. The nephew's name was Lee Harvey Oswald. The restaurant says Lee worked as a busboy but probably he was a numbers runner too.

New Orleans history is both wide AND deep...

Oct 26, 2018, 8:13 AM

It's just so weird to think that somewhere in this nation, there is a sweaty shadowy man sitting on his bed, watching the bulletins on the news and plotting his next maneuver. He means harm. He intends to inflict maximum pressure and pain on the American people. Only he knows his timing, when he will unleash his next wave of weapons on an unsuspecting populace. Only he knows what time the helicopter will take him to Andrews to board Air Force One.

Oct 27, 2018, 2:34 PM

The man who resurrected "America First" as a slogan, the slogan used in the Hitler days by isolationists and the American Nazi Party, today lectured the murdered Jews in the Pittsburgh synagogue on the shortcomings of their synagogue security and the evils of anti-
-Semitism.

Oct 27, 2018, 3:25 PM

First responders and their bosses do truly awesome work, but the post-gun-massacre press conference has taken on certain ritual Oscar-ish overtones that make me feel sick to my stomach. "First I'd like to thank..." Everyone knows and plays his or her part so comfortably. Everyone knows exactly what to do and say. Such a familiar ritual now.

Oct 29, 2018, 11:18 AM

"Today, Trump ate a baby on live television at his rally in Des Moines. Immediately the GOP responded by saying that it was not a real baby, it was a false flag baby, it was a Democratic baby, it was an immigrant baby, it was a member of MS-13 and ISIS. The baby is notorious. The baby attacked Trump first. The baby was a socialist and was quite delicious. Socialist babies are tasty but deceptive. At least Trump did not shoot anyone like that guy who shot Steve Scalise. Trump has done more to put food into the hands of babies and poor people than anyone ever in history."

Oct 29, 2018, 2:00 PM

Sarah Sanders just said that Trump was elected by "an overwhelming majority of 63 million American people."

She didn't mention that Hillary Clinton got 3 million more votes. This is the Bigliest Biggie Lie of the Trump presidency. The Founding Lie, the Original Lie, the lie upon which all the others are founded.

"Biggest crowds of any inauguration," he crowed. That was his first big public lie as president, and they're still telling it. They have now turned to Lying 24/7/365 as their only strategy. They lie when the truth would be easier! The Lie is now the point. "I am president* so I can tell you anything and make it true."

"Stick with me," he's saying, "I will LIE the white supremacist world into being. Just believe my lies and I'll take you with us. As long as you're white, straight, and Christian. Or rich and corrupt."

Oct 29, 2018, 10:38 PM

I am worried because the refugee caravan seems to be dwindling. If we are going to have taco trucks on every corner we are going to need a lot more folks.

Nov 2, 2018, 8:36 AM

Trump says if a refugee child throws a rock at a US soldier, she'll be shot. In other words, it's Friday morning in Trump's America, and the Geneva Convention is just a place Trump goes to rent porn stars.

Instead of spending $6,500,000 per day for soldiers to face down refugees, we could take the $1500 per day per refugee and put each one in a suite at the MGM Grand in Las Vegas. (Free buffet w/suite)

Nov 3, 2018, 11:15 AM

Something to Consider: The Trump you are seeing right now is the best performance Trump could put on for the midterms. This lying, racist demagogue of the thrice-daily insults, this incompetent wretch, this bully, is Trump desperately trying to convince you he is the right man for the job. This is Peak Trump.

Nov 5, 2018, 6:04 AM

Tomorrow marks a major showdown between Democratic voters and the people who don't know the difference between "your" and "you're."

Nov 6, 2018, 8:18 AM
[Once more into the 'Twas the Night breach]

'Twas the night before Midterms, when all thro' the House
No Republicans stirring - not even a Louse.
The migrants were hanged near the border with care
In hopes that my base voters might be found there

The Democrats nestled all snug in their beds,
While visions of Impeachment danced in their heads
And Mel in Laboutin, I in my hair-flap,
Had gone to our separate rooms for a nap

When out on the lawn, there arose such a clatter,
I sprang out of my bed to see what was the matter.
Away to the windows I trudged like a dolt

To confess all my crimes to good ol' Lester Holt

When, what to my wondering eyes should appear,
But a miniature sleigh, and eight tiny reindeer,
With a tall Negro driver, so slim and so quick,
It must be Obama! That guy makes me sick!

"Now! Biden, now! Tim Kaine! Now, Nancy Pelosi!
Who's that in the back? Wait now, let me go see!
On Michelle! John Lewis! On Valerie Jarrett!
On Beto O'Rourke! Give those reindeer a carrot!

To the top of the porch! To the top of the wall!
Now dash away! Dash away! Dash away all!"
And then in a twinkling, I heard on the roof
The prancing and pawing of each little hoof.

As I drew in my head, and was turning around,
Down the chimney, Saint Obama came with a bound
He wore a tan suit, from his head to his foot,
And some very cool shades on his head he had put,

Lots of government giveaways strapped to his back
He looked Presidential. Except he was black.
His eyes - how they twinkled! His dimples, so merry
They made me think of Sissy Spacek in "Carrie"

His expressive mouth was drawn up like a bow
And his once-dark black hair had gone white as snow
He spoke not a word, but went right to his work,
He emptied my stockings. He called me a jerk.

He said he would give all my gifts to the poor
And I owe the Treasury fifty million more,
Then, laying his finger aside of his nose,
And giving a nod, up the chimney he rose.

He sprang to his sleigh, to his team gave a whistle,
"Did you know Kim Jung-Un is building a new missile?"
But I heard him explain, ere he drove out of sight,
"There's a Blue Wave a-coming! It's coming tonight!"

Nov. 6, 2018 5:39 PM

Every time you see video of people standing in long lines to vote, you're witnessing voter suppression in action.

Nov 7, 2018, 8:37 AM

Trump says the midterm results are "tremendous." For once, I agree with him! Don't know about you, but this new, unsettled, rattled, furious, depressed, publicly unhinged Trump, totally off the rails, brought to you by our hard work and our votes - I like it!

Nov 9, 2018, 6:59 AM

I'm going to stake out a radical position here. I don't care what Jim Acosta said to Trump that people say was rude. I don't care what a showboat he is, or how obnoxious his questions might be. The First Amendment is designed to protect the most obnoxious questions on earth.

Trump's press-conference technique is to interrupt the questioner within the first few words, answer the question HE chooses to hear, blather on for a bit, then move along. He intentionally chooses reporters he doesn't like, provoking confrontation, hoping the hostile questions will redound to his credit with his fans.

The only way to pin him down is to repeat the question, more than once. He's so slippery you actually have to make him a bit mad to get him off his boilerplate lies to answer the damn question.

Acosta's questions are designed to make Trump reveal who he truly is. The president* almost came down off the podium and punched the reporter. That would have been even more instructive than his raging and lying. The unhinged Trump revealed by the press on Wednesday was the man with his mask stripped away. That's the reporter's job.

You don't defeat fascists by asking polite questions the way the fascists want them asked. You don't inform the public by accepting lies at face value. You can't be a good reporter if you want your subject to like you. I'm talking to you, Maggie Haberman.

Nov 9, 2018, 9:17 AM
Trump just illegally appointed an unqualified partisan hack named Matt Whitaker to be Acting Attorney General, and the Republicans are proving once more that they have the loudest crickets.

Nov 9, 2018, 11:21 AM
Every single time a mass shooter kills people, we ask "why" he did it. Law enforcement, media are obsessed with the question. What difference does it make? We always find out "why" but the shootings continue. "How" he did it is so much more important. HE DID IT WITH A GUN. Talk about the gun. Talk about how to stop him from getting a gun.

Nov 10, 2018, 7:16 AM
How would it be to wake up in burning California to see that people died in their cars fleeing the flames, and then to hear the president* of the United States blaming California Democrats for the wildfires?
No thoughts. No prayers. It's your fault, California. Shoulda voted for me.
The good news – No mass shooting last night!

Nov 10, 2018, 10:35 AM
Of course Trump canceled his cemetery visit to honor the WWI dead. It was raining and his hair is very blocky and uncooperative just now. Also, Jim Acosta was terribly rude to him this week. PLUS he had fire victims in California to insult. Lay off, libs!

Nov 10, 2018, 9:08 PM

FutureTweet™
Losers who attack me for skipping a Visit to the dead Army Men in pouring rain - Nothing to do with Hair Issues! I learned WWI was one

HUNDRED years ago - nobody who fought then is even ALIVE. They've all been dead a long time so really who cares? Live soldiers tell me, Sir, you're Great! Thanks for all your Doing! Fake News!

Nov 12, 2018, 3:57 PM

Reportedly Trump couldn't believe he won in November 2016. Maybe his deal with Putin called for him to lose. He seemed as shocked as anybody when he landed in the White House.

If Russian hackers did install Trump, I'm not sure even Robert Mueller will ever tell us so. I think he might just keep that one to himself rather than reveal to the world that the nightmarish last two years of our nation's history were nothing but a Russian counter-intelligence project.

Since November 2016 Trump has been trying to persuade us (and himself) that he really did win that election. He did it. All him. He brings it up in every speech - his "tremendous" victory, the "huge" inaugural crowds, the massive fantasy win in the popular vote brought on by three million imaginary caravan members swarming the polls in San Diego.

Over the past two years we've watched as he daily worked to convince us and himself that "the people" really love him - if they hadn't, how could he score such a massive (imaginary) victory over Hillary? His Rally Tour is just a ritual reenactment of the 2016 campaign, brought to 2018. Trump throwing "military parades" for himself every night. Imagine how sad and angry he is today - it's been more than a week since any crowd roared its approval of him! He must feel so low, like a junkie after a week without a needle. No wonder he cried and smashed all his toys on the trip to Paris.

The towering rage that erupted in public during that loony news conference is a sign. The rage has not abated. We did it, folks. We finally hurt Trump's feelings.

He said the midterm was all about him, and by God it was. For the first time since 2016, he learned in plain numbers that the whole "America loves me" fantasy has faded away like a porn star's kiss.

Nov 14, 2018, 7:50 AM

The next time Trump tells an African-American reporter she's "stupid," she should ask him to define the difference between the Baltics, the Balkans, Balzac, and his ballsack.

Or, if she's in a hurry, she can just ask, "Mr. President, who is currently the King of Africa?" and then wait.

Nov 16, 2018, 12:11 PM

Rich people get the most free stuff.

Nov 17, 2018, 9:33 AM

Trump is correct and our forests need more raking so I have bought a big rake, joined the Forest Rakers United Local 234, and I am headed West.

Mama, if I don't come back by winter, know that I died trying to rake out the 1,200,000 acres of forest in the Western United States, because that is how stupid I am willing to look to keep from admitting that mankind is changing the climate.

Nov 18, 2018, 6:45 PM
[On a visit to the site of California wildfires, Trump referred to the town of Paradise as "Pleasure."]

Constant raking our forests require,
Squads of rakists to stop forest fires.
Which is not to diminish
The ways of the Finnish
Paradise is not "Pleasure." Retire.

Nov 19, 2018, 8:50 AM

When I was eight years old I read a children's biography of Mozart that fascinated me. Mozart got incredibly rich and famous by the age of six by showing off his piano skills. I had taken only one year of piano lessons but I thought it possible I might also be a child prodigy.

To find out, I made a composing space out of some blankets behind the sofa and while my brothers watched "Batman" I composed a "symphony." It was about four pages long and written on real musical staff paper. If anybody bothered me I told them to go away, I was writing a symphony. I composed it entirely in my head as I read that's how Mozart worked.

When my Opus One was finished I took the pages to the piano and picked it out. I don't remember how bad it was. It was not good enough for me to ever try composing again or even playing it again. I went back to playing the "Gone With the Wind" theme real loud for my Mom. She liked it more than my symphony. Sure, you can do anything - but it's good to find out at an early age that ambition has limits.

Nov 20, 2018, 6:31 PM

It's a great thing our government can leap into action and get all the romaine lettuce removed from store shelves to stop a salmonella outbreak. But last I checked nobody had used any romaine to kill a bunch of people in a hospital, a country-music bar, a Las Vegas concert, or a synagogue.

Nov 23, 2018, 4:27 PM

Happy Thanksgiving! Trump says the thing he is most thankful for is Trump, so that makes one of us.

Nov 23, 2018, 8:23 PM

Upon a Photograph of the Trumps at Thanksgiving Dinner

How miserable they look. Insulting all your friends and enemies on Twitter isn't as much fun as it used to be. Sticking it to other people doesn't bring a lot of smiles to these faces. She's thinking about her boyfriend. The room is ugly and smells of gravy, smells of rotten old people who pay $200,000 a year to sit in this tacky mausoleum and eat from a buffet. The couple sits apart, behind a velvet rope, on better chairs than the chairs given to the $200,000 people.

Nov 26, 2018, 8:50 AM

Trump changed the rules as the asylum-seekers approached the border. He's slow-walking the asylum procedures, processing fewer than 50 refugees per day. He's doing this in order to create a crisis, to frustrate the refugees in attempting to cross, as they did yesterday.

Many online Trump supporters celebrated the gassing of children and said they wished it was bullets instead of gas.

The media goes about their business doing happy holiday feature stories while our government goes off the rails. When Trump first took office, a story like this would have sent hundreds of thousands of people into the streets in protest. I want to make a sign and go protest somewhere. I worry that he's wearing us down.

Nov 26, 2018, 10:43 AM
[Melania poses with her crimson Christmas trees]

I walk in lonely coat
through car wash of desertion
waiting for Secret Service kisses
to ease pain of me.

Nov 27, 2018, 7:40 AM

Trump says his trade war has nothing to do with General Motors closing 5 plants and putting 15,000 people out of work. He told GM chairman Mary Barra to "make a better car."

Imagine a Trump-designed car - 6 tons, gold-plated, V-28 engine, 50 gallons to the mile, twin smokestacks. Built-in toilet. Inflatable pornstar airbags. No bumpers, no seatbelts, no safety equipment. Roof-mounted AR-15s. Teargas ventilation. Heavy and slow - the largest lemon in the world! List price $6.3 million (discount to MAGA hat wearers).

Get it now, folks, the 2019 Trump Fiasko! Like a Bus crossed with a Hummer - it's a Bummer!

Nov 27, 2018, 3:31 PM

"I remember I met Elvis, big strong man, and he was crying, and he said, 'Sir, I just want to thank you for everything you've done, you look more like me than I do, Sir, and I just want to say you are welcome to get up onto my blue suede shoes any time, Sir.' He told me that."

Nov 28, 2018, 9:25 AM

Trump: "I have a gut, and my gut tells me more sometimes than anybody else's brain can ever tell me."

You have to admit, that is quite a gut.

Nov 29, 2018, 7:12 AM

Trump fled the White House Christmas tree lighting ceremony in such haste that it was rumored he had a panic attack, but no, he was just hurrying back to the White House in time to see himself on live TV.

Nov 29, 2018, 3:08 PM

My mockery of Melanie's menstrual trees made the "Today" show roundup of Melania mockery. I'm delighted. Not just because the show's commenters get many chances to destroy me online (and to announce that Melanie's red trees are meant to symbolize the deployed soldier, or some such late-invented bilge) - but also this brings me just one step closer to my life dream of being blocked by an actual Trump.

Nov 29, 2018, 5:40 PM

When the singer's your pal, Michael Cohen,
It seems prison is where you'll be going
Try not to be bitter
We'll let you have Twitter
And your wife can go back to her hoeing

Dec 1, 2018, 7:39 AM
[The death of former President George H.W. Bush is announced.]

Uh-oh. I am guessing that protocol will dictate that you-know-who has to attend Bush's funeral.

A: He really wants to come show his respects
B: That's fine, he is the president* and it's a state funeral, that's expected
A: He wants to call the old man "Low Energy Bush" in the eulogy
B: That will not be acceptable
A: Okay, what if he live-tweets a mild insult of Jeb at the funeral
B: They're not going to go for that
A: We need to know if there is any possibility of rain, any possibility at all. The hair
B: Anything's possible
A: He's planning to wear golf clothes and go straight to his club from the church
B: Yeah we expected that

Meanwhile in the Residence:

T: But I don't WANT to I HATE funerals everybody is so SAD
S: But afterward you can have 3 scoops of ice cream
T: How many does everybody else get?
S: Everybody else just gets 1 scoop
T: I want 4 scoops

Dec 2, 2018, 9:58 AM

Trump's Sunday Schedule:

8-9 am Ride the horsey
9-10 am Sesame Street
10-10:15 am Snack (graham crackers and milk)
10:15-11 am Shapes and Colors
11-11:30 am Nap time
11:30-12 pm Clean up, wipe up, didy
12-1 pm Executive Time

1-3 pm Afternoon tantrum
3-3:15 pm Medication time with Dr. Ronny
3:15-5 pm Cocaine Therapy
5-6 Executive Time
6-6:15 pm Didy
6:15-9 pm Evening tantrum

Dec 2, 2018, 10:40 AM
If anyone within the sound of my voice is a great painter in oils, please paint a monumental canvas entitled "Trump Received By Buchanan and Hoover Upon Entering the Heaven of Bad Presidents"

Dec 3, 2018, 9:18 AM
Imagine, if you will, that it was Trump and not GHW Bush who died on Friday. Imagine having to write a gracious statement about that event.

"Whatever else he was, Trump, was, above all else, indisputably, incontrovertibly, himself."

"Trump didn't bother with the small stuff, such as 'how an umbrella works" or 'which other countries exist,' but he could always be counted upon for a good anecdote about one of his triumphs."

"In a world full of leaders, Donald Trump stood out -- but never in the rain."

"He was one of America's most recent presidents."

"Love him or loathe him, you had to admit the man had a massive number of Twitter followers."

Dec 4, 2018, 7:34 AM
Dan Quayle has announced that George HW Bush was "my hero." (A joke for Democrats of a certain age.)

Dec 14, 2018, 1:36 PM

"ADDERALL" Scene 1
EXT. WHITE HOUSE - NIGHT

Deep in the early hours. In the family quarters, a lone lightbulb burns. We hear a rhythmic tapping, the sound of a plastic straw scraping a tabletop. A massive sniff.

BARRON
Mr. Trump?

TRUMP
Go back to bed!

BARRON
But it's that guy - that Russian! He wants to Facetime you on my laptop again…

TRUMP
Oh f*(k. Okay. I'll be right there. (sniff)

Dec 19, 2018, 7:42 AM
     I know somebody whose charitable foundation was not shut down yesterday because courts determined it was a fraud and a criminal conspiracy against the United States. Her name is Hillary Clinton.

Dec 20, 2018, 4:33 PM
     The wheels are off the bus. The shit has hit the fan. The walls are closing in. This is the end of the beginning. He's in the biggest rage he's ever been in since the last rage. The chickens are coming home to roost. The fat lady has begun to sing. It's when the jungle drums stop that you have to worry. It ain't over till it's over. The rats are rearranging the deck chairs on the Titanic. The only thing worse than this is the next thing. His advisors are deeply concerned. Republicans are deeply concerned. Democrats are deeply concerned. His family is deeply

concerned. His dog would be deeply concerned but he does not have a dog because he does not like dogs and DOGS DO NOT LIKE HIM.

Dec 21, 2018, 10:37 AM
Sung lustily to the tune of "Santa, Baby"

Bobby baby, new indictments under the tree for me
Been an awful good boy
Bobby baby, and hurry that grand jury tonight

Bobby baby, indict a family member or two - boohoo
We've been patient so long
Bobby baby, so hurry up your lawyers tonight

Bobby baby, I want a perp walk and really that's not a lot
Been an angel all year
Bobby baby, so hurry those subpoenas tonight

Bobby honey, one thing I really do need, decreed
By a federal judge
Bobby baby, so hurry with the handcuffs tonight!

Bobby cutie, fill my stocking with balances - and checks
Sign your X on the line
Bobby cutie, and put a Trump in prison tonight....

Lock 'em up and lose the key
(All except poor Tiffany)
I really do believe in you
Let's see if you believe in me

Bobby baby, forgot to mention one little thing: Sing-Sing
I don't mean like a song
Bobby baby, so hurry down the chimney tonight!
Hurry down the chimney tonight!
Hurry, tonight

Dec 23, 2018, 5:11 PM

Those hailing the departing General Mattis will soon realize that "the adult in the room" just left our nuclear missiles in the hands of a psychotic three-year-old.

Dec 26, 2018, 8:34 AM

Merry Christmas, Happy Government Shutdown!

Why does the news media ALWAYS fail to mention that Republicans are the party that shuts down the government every time?

Dec. 26, 2018

This is not one of my inventions: this is directly from the transcript of Trump's video Christmas message to the US troops serving overseas.

"It's like — take another example. Take Comey. Everybody hated Comey. They thought he did a horrible job. The Democrats hated him. Literally, the day before I fired him, they were saying he should be fired. As soon as I fired him, they said, "Oh, what did you fire him for? That was a terrible thing to do." It's a disgrace what's happening in our country.

"But other than that, I wish everybody a very merry Christmas. Thank you very much. Thank you."

Dec 27, 2018, 9:50 AM

Trump says most of the people furloughed during the government shutdown are Democrats. What goes unremarked, day after day, is how strange it is for the majority of us to live in a nation where we are openly despised by the president*.

Dec 28, 2018, 8:01 AM

I was just thinking about Eleanor Rosalynn Smith Carter. They made a lot of fun of her as First Lady, her honeyed accent and her bashful ways. In the 38 years since her husband left office, she has been there at every Sunday School class and Habitat for Humanity house-build, every trip to an African nation to fight river blindness. Jimmy gets all the credit for his post-presidency but folks always forget to mention Rosalynn. I wish we could elect her President, just for a while. I bet she'd be our wisest president ever.

Dec 28, 2018, 5:18 PM

Hey Trump: Don't close Border. Don't build Wall. Don't emit Whine. Don't excrete Lie. Don't MAGA. Don't insult Ally. Don't stroke Enemy. Don't betray Country. Don't imprison Baby. Don't hate Muslim. Don't grab Pussy. Don't kill Refugee. Don't coddle Murderer. JUST DON'T.

Dec 28, 2018, 6:19 PM

If you're at your parents' house and sick of hearing Fox News, just go into their cable settings and block the channel. They don't know how to unblock. That's why the setting is known as "parental controls."

2019

Jan 1, 2019 8:44 AM
We usually say "Happy" but we get the gist.

 Melania Trump ✔ @FLOTUS · 4m
#HappNewYear2019 ✨

Jan. 1, 2019 9:01 AM

Hitler, Mussolini, Stalin, Mao: all the great authoritarians had an enormous opinion of themselves, and proclaimed themselves not only Very Stable Geniuses but demigods. The biggest difference between Trump and those dudes is his utter, unfailing incompetence. May it finally lead to his downfall in 2019!

Jan 1, 2019, 6:56 PM

The next time somebody tells you "experience" is the most important quality in a Democratic nominee, you can point out that every winning Democrat since JFK has been the candidate with LESS experience.

JFK, Carter, Clinton, Obama. All "inexperienced." All younger than their opponent. All charismatic. All winners.

Jan 5, 2019, 11:54 AM

Everybody got all mad at freshman Rep. Rashida Tlaib for calling Trump a "motherfucker," but nobody had any doubt which mother-fucker she was talking about.

Jan 5, 2019, 8:53 PM

Fuming, belching, watching Fox, he lets his mind drift back to a simpler time when a pretty girl spanked him with a copy of Forbes that had his face on it.

He slumped against the mound of pillows. It was vitally important to get the diaper off himself before the valet arrived to help him shower and dress. It still felt important to change his own diaper. Show 'em who's boss, he thought. Show 'em who's president.

Jan 6, 2019, 1:15 PM

It's a Witch Hunt so when is it time to find out if he floats or sinks? Because I'm pretty sure he will float, and you know what that means.

Jan 7, 2019, 11:09 AM
Looking for a way to make Daddy love me a little less.

[Photo: Instagram/IvankaTrump]

Jan 8, 2019, 7:26 PM
We have obtained advance text of the president's* remarks but have not been able to determine their validity:

"My fellow Americans, I am the greatest fraud ever perpetrated on the United States of America. I am a tool of Vladimir Putin. I commit crimes like a dog humps a pillow. My hair is spun fresh every morning from seedy garbage by a platoon of flatulent robots. I snort. I sniff. I kick my own ass. I am not only my own worst enemy but yours as well. My wife is quickly becoming a hag despite the best efforts of modern chemists and engineers. A pig would be angry to wake up and be me. I am having a crisis in the back of my pants."

Jan 9, 2019, 7:25 AM
Actual post from AP Politics on Twitter:

"AP FACT CHECK: Democrats put the blame for the shutdown on Trump. But it takes two to tango. Trump's demand for $5.7 billion for his border wall is one reason for the budget impasse. The Democrats' refusal to approve the money is another."

Hmmm ... "AP FACT CHECK: Americans put the blame for the assassination on Oswald. But it takes two to tango. Lee Harvey Oswald firing a rifle at the motorcade is one reason for the President's murder. JFK's insistence on coming to Dallas is another."

Jan 9, 2019, 7:31 PM

Oh yes sir Yes yes yes you were Great Greatest presidential address EVER Sir Yes your phrases were silken Yes this will really do the trick Oh yes SIR we are getting calls of praise and admiration Indeed sir fine that was a FINE speech sir that was BRILLIANT no leader SINCE CHURCHILL

Jan 10, 2019, 12:15 PM

Yes he is a good boy yes he is!
Wall
Look how he ate all his peas
Wall!
Sit up nice and tall in your chair, darling
WALL
Had a nice nap, now he's all clean
WALL! WALL! WALL!
What is it, honey? You want your toy?
WALLLLLLLL! WALLLLLLLL!
Use your words, honey
WAAAAAAAAAAAAAAAAAAAAAAAAAAAAA

Jan 10, 2019, 12:50 PM
"The buck stops with everyone"
"Give me liberty or give me a bucket of fried chicken"
"December 7, 1941, a day that was all the Democrats' fault"
"That's one small step for a man, probably a hoax"

"I regret that I have but one country to sell in my lifetime"

Jan 12, 2019, 9:10 PM

WHEN YOU CAN'T SAY 'NO'

PIRRO: "Are you now or have you ever worked for Russia, Mr. President?"

TRUMP: "I think it's the most insulting thing I've ever been asked... If you read the article, you'll find they had nothing... It's called the failing New York Times for a reason..."

Jan 14, 2019, 8:57 PM
Trump ordered hamburgers for the Clemson football team. Because highly-trained athletes love to eat chemical-laden fast food.

Jan 17, 2019, 6:37 PM
[First report of Trump's attempts to extort the leaders of Ukraine into investigating Joe Biden, his main opponent]

If Nancy Pelosi can effect the peaceful removal of Donald Trump from the presidency, she will go down in history as the greatest American ever. And we will build a monument to celebrate her.

Jan 18, 2019, 6:35 PM

For two years now, hardcore Democrats have been railing at each other about impeachment, when nobody outside our Circle of Outrage seemed to be much interested in what that Chickenfucker was doing to our country. Now everyone in the world is talking impeachment. It's the word on every pair of lips. I feel myself relaxing just a bit. I now dare to believe Trump has crested Mt. Karma at last and is beginning his long, long hike down the back slope.

Jan 26, 2019, 3:30 AM

CNN: Trump caves, Stone arrested
MSNBC: Trump caves, Stone arrested
CNBC: Trump caves, Stone arrested
FOX: Huma Abedin conspired with Alexandra Ocasio-Cortez to steal Hillary's emails from Q-Anon pizza parlor

Jan 26, 2019, 5:49 PM

When dealing with Nancy Pelosi
Trump must feel a certain jelosi
She simply said No
To her imbecile foe
And his poll numbers went to hellosi

Jan 30, 2019, 6:08 PM

Sarah Sanders on the Christian Broadcasting Network: "God wanted Donald Trump to become President."

God also wants people to have two eyes that look straight ahead, but what are you gonna do?

Jan 31, 2019, 12:07 PM

The fact that some people have billions - in a world where many people have not a dollar to their name - is the surest sign that our system is broken, corrupt, and disgusting. Instead of electing billionaires to office, we should be turning them back into millionaires and giving their excess wealth to starving people.

What if we took away all of Mark Zuckerberg's wealth except for $100 million - and divided the remaining 70 billion + change among all Americans? Each of us would get a check for approximately $201. Doesn't that sound like a good idea? What a nice dinner we can have! And Zuckerberg will still have a hundred mil, so he won't have to associate with the huddled masses.

Feb 6, 2019, 7:56 PM

"From the fusky golden trapezoids of Eastern Montana, to the buxom volcanic cones of Far South Florida - from the blue-green fir thickets of central Utah to the hideous blackberry maelstrom of West Dakota, the state of our Onion is strong - strong like the five-year-old Limburger cheese. Strong like the socks of the athlete marinated in a spittoon of sauerkraut. Strong, my fellow Americans, like the rank disapproval of my many, many men enemies, whom I like to call, my Menemies." - From the State of the Onion address 2019

Feb 10, 2019, 11:15 AM

Media: Elizabeth Warren, Kamala Harris, Amy Klobuchar are unlikable liars.

Also media: guess what crazy outrageous zany stuff the president* said about POCAHONTAS today, you won't believe this one!!!

Feb 12, 2019, 3:40 PM

Trump is trying to explain why he doesn't have a dog, but the truth is all the dogs in the world voted to shun him. Even the Russian wolfhound voted against him. The movement is apparently being led by a pack of unruly Corgis in the west of England.

Trump says it would be "phony" for him to have a dog. He's right. Dogs know.

Feb 13, 2019, 6:29 AM

One of the most common forms of crime here in New Orleans is homeless-on-homeless assault. The chirpy TV news reader just announced the murder of a "beloved homeless man" who "lived under the Claiborne Avenue flyover."

Can any homeless person be described as "beloved?" If he was beloved, why didn't someone give him a place to live?

When I was a young reporter at the *Birmingham News* in 1977, my editor sent me out to Brookwood Mall to interview a man who was living in a cardboard box on a hill above the mall. That's how unusual homelessness was, in 1977. The story made the front page of the newspaper.

How did we become a country that turns away from homeless people? Why can't we just give them homes? We're the richest nation on earth. Why should anyone's address be "under the Claiborne Avenue flyover?" Our country is just so weird. We want to build walls to keep poor people out, but we can't even take care of the people living under the freeway.

Feb 15, 2019, 10:12 AM

Minutes after declaring a "national emergency," Trump says, "I could do the wall over a longer period of time. I didn't need to do this, but I'd rather do it much faster." Then he rushed to Mar-A-Lago to play 18 holes. Folks, what we have is a Nationalist Emergency.

Feb 16, 2019, 8:49 AM

Just checking in SAFE - thank God I'm still alive on Day #2 of the National Emergency! My home is surrounded by taco trucks. Small children keep asking if I am their Papi. An SUV full of MS-13 just careened past firing Mexican guns. Everybody stay safe!

Feb 20, 2019, 2:16 PM

Surviving this national emergency
Devoid of the slightest real urgency
Means we resist calls
For ridiculous Walls
While we choose one to lead the insurgency

Feb 20, 2019, 9:33 PM
The main thing to remember about the Jussie Smollett scandal is that the president* of the United States is an active Russian asset working to shut down all investigations into his many impeachable acts.

Feb 21, 2019, 7:36 AM
Another thing to remember about the Jussie Smollett controversy is that a white nationalist Trump supporter in the Coast Guard amassed a huge arsenal and planned to kill prominent liberal politicians and media figures - but if you watch NBC you'd think he was just targeting "politicians."

Feb 22, 2019, 7:18 AM

Those tiresome tweets from Ivanka
Remind me her dad wants to spanka

Feb 25, 2019, 11:25 AM
Trump is so racist that when Spike Lee calls for people to "do the right thing" and vote, Trump thinks that's a slur against white people. Which, maybe it is.

Feb 27, 2019, 8:44 PM
If a president cannot be indicted he's a king.

Mar 1, 2019, 7:27 AM

'Twas not a great week for the Don man
His fixer confirmed he's a con man
Don sucked up to Kim
Walked out on a whim -
Let's bring on the big denouement, man

Mar 4, 2019, 6:55 AM

"I am an innocent man" - Trump

"I am an expert skeet shooter" - Helen Keller

"I am a gentle artist, a bon vivant, a man of peace" - Adolf Hitler

"Both my eyes are looking at the same thing at once" - Sarah Sanders

Mar 6, 2019, 8:02 AM
    Roger Stone came to Mardi Gras this year.

Mar 7, 2019, 9:30 AM

"Sir, we don't use cages for children. Sir, they're not cages," said Homeland Security Secretary Krijsten Nielsen.

Congressman Bennie Thomas (D-MS) asked what they are, if not cages.

They are "areas of the border facility that are carved out for the safety and protection of those who remain there while they're being processed," Nielsen said.

Rep. Bonnie Watson Coleman (D-NJ) asked again what a chain--link enclosure on concrete floor is, if it is not a cage.

"It's a detention space, as you know, that has existed for decades. It's larger. It has facilities. There are places to sit, to stand, to lay down."

"So does my dog's cage," Watson Coleman responded.

Don't call them cages.
Call them what they are:
Learning Enclosures.
Motion-Calming Discipline Cubes.
Corrective Eight-Walled Openspaces.
Childhood Spatial-Tactile Exploration Experiences.
Pan-Cultural Geometry-Teaching Devices.
After extensive marketing studies we have chosen:
"Welcome Home" ChildBox™

Mar 7, 2019, 6:21 PM

The fix is in. Prosecutors asked for 19 years for Manafort. The judge gave him 47 months and said he had lived an otherwise "blameless life." This after Manafort lied to everyone and has never expressed one moment of remorse for his crimes. This is the Republican corrupted judiciary in action, the Trump autocracy coming to full boil. Stop putting your faith in Mueller.

Mar 12, 2019, 7:01 AM

One handy thing about being the worst human being in the world is that you and all your friends can be revealed to have hung out with the queen of south Florida strip-mall human-trafficking sex parlors, and everybody shrugs and says "what else ya got?"

Mar 15, 2019, 5:06 PM

Happy fifteenth of March to our Caesar
Our orange, malevolent geezer
If you have a minute
Please drop by the Senate
That would be a real people-pleaser

Mar 18, 2019, 11:58 AM

It was September 23, 1975, two days after my eighteenth birthday. I was managing editor of the Crimson White, the student newspaper at the University of Alabama. Nobody else wanted to cover the press conference of the former governor of California, who was running in the 1976 Republican primary for president. I volunteered.

Ronald Reagan showed up by himself, no security, driving his own rental car. He wore a tuxedo because he was speaking later at a fundraiser at the North River Yacht Club.

No other reporters showed up for his press conference. This didn't seem to bother him. He shrugged, smiled, and said, "Know where we can get a cup of coffee?" I led him across the quad to the Kwik Snak. He ordered coffee and a grilled cheese sandwich. I had a Coke. The news was full of the previous day's assassination attempt by Sara Jane Moore on Gerald Ford. I got Reagan to say on the record that he wouldn't be for any form of gun control no matter who got shot at. (The AP picked up the quote! I was thrilled.) Reagan also said off the record that Ford wouldn't be president much longer. He said HE would win. He was four years early with his prediction, but he did turn out to be right.

Everything you've heard about his charm was true. I was never tempted to vote for him but I was happy to sit and listen to his stories at the Kwik Snak.

Mar 19, 2019, 1:11 PM

John McCain used to be the Republican example of an American hero. Now the only Republican I hear defending him against Trump's posthumous slanders is his daughter. Guess Trump has grabbed them all by the pussy, huh.

Mar 20, 2019, 10:34 PM

Trump is fighting a man who's been dead for seven months. And the dead man is winning.

Mar 21, 2019, 9:50 AM

AT LAST McCAIN'S THANK-YOU NOTE ARRIVES

Dear Don,

It comes to my attention that you did not receive my thank-you note for my funeral. I have been busy being dead since then, and apologize for the oversight.

The service was awesome. Where were you? We missed you! Oh that's right, you were the only one not invited.

In your head, always, always,

John McCain

Mar 22, 2019, 4:47 PM

Breaking: Table of contents, Mueller Report
1. Guilty
2. Guilteeeehhhh
3. Guilterino
4, Guilt-O-Matic
5. Guiltappotamus
6. Guiltawithtonic
7. Guiltaguiltaguiltaohyehbaby
8. Guilticulously Guiltabulous Guilteronomous
9. Guuuiiiiiiillllllllllltttttttttttyyyyyyyyyyyyyyyyyyyyyyy

Mar 22, 2019, 7:29 PM
Maybe the dog ate Mueller's homework.

Mar 23, 2019, 7:31 AM
Stayed up all night to sift through all the reporting on the Mueller report. Apparently Mueller will report that not only did Trump commit no crime, he's a really nice guy, sweet-natured, even-tempered, with a firm grasp of issues and innate sympathy for the feelings of others - honest as the day is long, the healthiest human being ever elected, loves and is loved by all dogs and kitties, musically gifted, heckuva dancer, really good with small children, secretly gives anonymous millions to poor people, and has gigantic hands. Hands so big. Hands as big as Russia.

Mar 24, 2019, 10:25 PM
Bill Clinton obstructed justice by saying "there is no affair."
The United States House of Representatives *impeached* him for the crime of obstructing justice.
...but Trump surrogates had dozens of meetings with Russians, Trump fired the FBI director and Attorney General and said he did it to stop their investigations of him, Trump Jr and campaign staff met secretly with Russian spies and lied about it, 34 people were indicted for lying about something that we are now told never happened, Trump lied about Trump Moscow right up until now, and he is *exonerated?*
And there was no crime? Except the 34 people indicted for lying? About something that did not happen?

Mar 26, 2019, 11:36 AM
Just in, a new summary from Attorney General William Barr:
"The investigation has not been able to establish that the female subject, JULIET CAPULET, was in fact a minor at the time of the alleged wedding, and although ROMEO MONTAGUE has admitted to multiple acts of collusion with JULIET CAPULET while under the impression that she was in fact a minor, we find insufficient reason to prosecute him for possible involvement in her death, which seems to

have been her decision alone. This is neither an indictment of ROMEO MONTAGUE nor an exoneration."

Mar 26, 2019, 9:32 PM
JUST IN: Barr releases Mueller report

Mar 27, 2019, 9:46 AM

Biden's too old. Bernie Sanders is, too.
Amy's too mean. Beto's shirt is too blue.
Elizabeth Warren's much smarter than I,
Booker's too old to be a single guy.
Gillibrand? No, I'm an Al Franken fan.
Kamala? Too prosecutorial, man!
Hickenlooper? Castro? Buttigieg? Wow!
Voters will learn to pronounce them somehow.
Any one of these is much better, by far,
Than the man who applies yellow hair from a jar.

Mar 29, 2019, 8:08
    The only people fighting to keep you from seeing the Mueller report are the people claiming the report is a "complete and total exoneration" of Trump. Hmmm what's up with that do you think?

Mar 31, 2019, 10:20 AM

Dear Betsy deVos,

Your boss just set you up and used you big time. Insisted that you cut Special Olympics, got you to go out and defend that action, then Trump squashed it and took credit for saving America from you, Cruella deVos. From your point of view, does this feel like winning?

Asking for 65 million friends.

Apr 1, 2019, 9:09 AM

If the Mueller report really exonerated Trump, Fox News would be reading it aloud, line by line.

Apr 2, 2019, 3:02 PM

25th Amendment update: The man who holds the nuclear codes tried three times today to say the word "origins," but it came out "oranges." Finally he just switched to "beginnings." My mother made a lot of these mistakes early in her dementia, when she was trying to hide it from everybody.

Apr 4, 2019, 8:19 AM

Trump strikes back against the elites:

"My father came from humble oranges. He was a poor hamberder from Germany, the awesomest part of Germany. He fled the horrible whining sound of those deadly windmills and came here to evade the draft and to seek a job running a whorehouse."

Apr 4, 2019, 8:41 PM

Yes, hello? I should like to enlist in the Army of Presidential Harassment where we live in tents, sing campfire songs, and devote every waking hour to making his day as bad as it can possibly be.

Yes, my darlin' mother, the boys of Oh-nineteen
Are camped out by the freeway, we're sharpening our memes
We're takin' back our country, Ma, the way you'd have us do
And we'll put all the Trumps in jail by twenty-twenty-two"

- Trad. camp song, Army of Presidential Harassment

Apr 5, 2019, 2:38 PM

The next Democratic nominee has a difficult job. She has to knit together our fractious coalition, inspire a wave of new voters, fend off the toxic fascist assaults of the Russia Party, and somehow lead America out of the worst mess we've faced since Pearl Harbor.

We can't settle for somebody who "deserves" the nomination. Or someone who checks all our issue boxes. Or someone who seems "electable." And we can't just wish her into being. (Or him.)

Apr 6, 2019, 3:52 PM

The Republicans wouldn't mind saving the earth if there was any money in it.

Apr 6, 2019, 7:50 PM

Caution: Do not take PROTRUDA™ if you are allergic to it, which you can find out by taking PROTRUDA™. If you survive, you are not allergic to PROTRUDA™ and may continue to take it. In some cases, sudden death, long lingering painful death, suicide, matricide, patricide, and regicide have occurred. Results not typical. If you experience a god-like euphoria followed by a sparkly fading sense of philosophical letdown, discontinue use and contact your physician.

Apr 8, 2019, 7:29 AM

Trump fired Kirstjen Nielsen as Secretary of Homeland Security because she refused to close the border. Because she wasn't breaking the law enthusiastically enough. Because putting kids in cages and losing track of them wasn't mean enough. He wants tear gas and bullets and bodies. He promised a crisis at the southern border and BY GOD he intends to deliver. He doesn't intend to let ANY law stand in his way.

Apr 8, 2019, 7:30 PM

Trump told his Border Patrol agents to ignore any judge who tells them they can't block asylum seekers from entering the United States.

Trump, in his official position as leader of the executive branch, ordered our federal employees to violate the laws and do what he tells them instead. No Republican has lifted a finger to stop him, or even spoken out against him.

Apr 9, 2019, 8:05 AM
I am now writing chyrons for Fox News.

WHAT DOES RACISM LOOK LIKE?
· TUCKER CARLSON tonight · #Tucker

Apr 9, 2019, 9:36 PM
I was born in 1957 at the height of the baby boom, at the very farthest left the political pendulum ever swung in this country. Maybe that's why I've lived my life in a state of accelerating disbelief. Politically, the USA has been moving to the right since the day I was born. Moving away from the triumphant Democratic liberalism of Kennedy, Johnson and my childhood, moving ever rightward. Away from the brand-new interstates and airports and schools, the miracle of the polio vaccine, the miracles of science and space and medicine and good government. Moving toward the past.

If this country moves any more to the right we will fall off the edge of the flat earth.

Apr 10, 2019, 11:24 AM
Like Charles A. Lindbergh, Attorney General Bill Barr is the kind of fascist who looks perfectly reasonable at first glance.

Apr 11, 2019, 9:35 AM

Leo Tolstoy was 82 years old when he finally got fed up with his wife Sofia. He was becoming increasingly ascetic, and had given up the royalties to his books so that he could live more like a peasant. This didn't sit well with Sofia. Finally, Leo had had enough. Fleeing home, wife, and wealth, he set off on an epic train journey trying to find his freedom. He fell to pneumonia in a remote countryside train station. The station became the center of Russia's first media firestorm. Eight days later Tolstoy died in the stationmaster's house.

Apr 12, 2019, 8:12 AM

It takes a certain kind of guts to rail against "socialism" while handing the country over to Russia. It's the kind of thing you can only do if:

Hatred is your brand.
Cruelty is your brand.
Ignorance is your brand.
Incompetence is your brand.
Corruption is your brand.
Amorality is your brand.
Belligerence is your brand.
Misogyny is your brand.
Racism is your brand.
Hostility is your brand.
Aggression is your brand.

Apr 14, 2019, 12:51 PM

Trump rage-tweeted all night. Must be mad he's not down at Mar-A-Lago getting his stripmall handjob, selling twenty-dollar secrets to his old-lady Chinese spy friends, and cheating his sycophants at golf games they're paid to play with him.

Apr 14, 2019, 10:20 PM

I am inclined to support Pete Buttigieg because he's so smart and has that indefinable quality we call "charisma." But I am a realist, too.

I didn't know how much white America hates black people until Obama. I didn't know how much male America hates women leaders until Hillary. And I'm afraid that if Pete succeeds, as much as I wish it could happen, we will discover how America really feels about us queers.

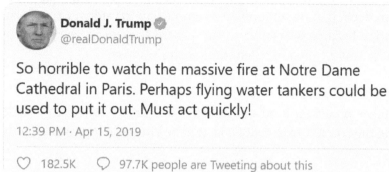

Donald J. Trump ✓
@realDonaldTrump

So horrible to watch the massive fire at Notre Dame Cathedral in Paris. Perhaps flying water tankers could be used to put it out. Must act quickly!

12:39 PM · Apr 15, 2019   ⓘ

♡ 182.5K   💬 97.7K people are Tweeting about this

Apr 15, 2019, 1:10 PM
Fire-homme Marcel: What do you think we should do?
Fire-homme Pierre: Mon dieu, I have no idea!
M: Check the Trump feed!
P: He proposes flying water tankers! Sacre bleu!
M: Brilliant! We shall design and build some soon!
P: But he says we must ACT QUICKLY!
M: Why?
P: Unsure, perhaps because Notre Dame she is burning now
M: Let's take his great advice! Design and build those tankers! TOUT SUITE!!

Apr 16, 2019, 1:13 PM
Why don't Democrats nominate a Roomba robotic vacuum cleaner? Then we can just program in the qualities and identities we want our nominee to have. Our nominee can bump into walls and go under sofas and clean up Trump's mess.

All our human candidates have flaws, but robots are perfect. No machine has ever made a misteak. With Roomba as our nominee, we won't have to argue about the stupid flaws of real people. We can just send our robot out to do battle with Trump. Our robot can be female, male, gay, straight, black, white, AND Native American. Moderate and wildly progressive. Hip and square. All without breaking a sweat. Roomba 2020! Humans bad! Robots good!

Apr 16, 2019, 7:57 PM
I have pairs of socks that are older and have been together longer than Pete and Chasten Buttigieg.

Apr 17, 2019, 1:40 PM
I think the perfect way to cover Columbine would be to quietly, respectfully ignore the "anniversary." When did we start celebrating anniversaries of horrific crimes? What difference does it make that it's 20 years? A year is a number of days based (sort of) on the earth's orbit around the sun, and "20" is no more significant a number than 19 or 18.

The "anniversary" is an excuse for TV to gin up its horror machine and run all that terrible video again, on the pretext of "remembering." Let's put all the survivors through the trauma again, so we can get some of that delicious video in this segment!

What it has done and will do is inspire copycats. I'll bet everybody within five miles of Columbine High wishes the media would just shut up about it.

Apr 18, 2019, 9:35 AM
Lackey Bill Barr said the POTUS* did not obstruct justice because he was frustrated and angered by the investigation and had a "sincere belief" that it was unfair. Let's call this the Trump Baby Defense.

Mueller: "Here are 10 episodes of Trump obstructing justice."
Barr: "Nope."

Apr 18, 2019, 4:29 PM
I spent an afternoon reading the Mueller report. (Full disclosure: I didn't read all the footnotes.) It is a book-length catalogue of corrupt behavior. It's all there: 445 pages of obstructive, collusive, conspiratorial actions. High crimes. Misdemeanors. Let's remember that Bill

Clinton was impeached simply for saying "there IS no affair." That was his crime.

Either Trump must be impeached, or we might as well take impeachment out of the Constitution and buy the king a golden crown.

Apr 18, 2019, 5:35 PM

I'm no lawyer, but it looks like the only way Donald Trump Jr. could have been indicted is if his email said "If it's what you say, I like it. Especially later in the summer. Also, I AM FULLY AWARE THAT I AM COMMITTING A CRIME BY HAVING THIS MEETING."

Apr 19, 2019, 11:53 AM

Sen. Kamala Harris came to New Orleans this morning, giving speeches and raising money. I begged entrance to a gathering for her at Dooky Chase, the most famous African-American restaurant in New Orleans and a must-stop for all politicians.

At first glance: Harris is smaller, funnier, and warmer than she appears on television. She delivered a brief version of her standard pitch, I'm sure, but made it feel as if she was speaking off the cuff. The theme was "Let's speak the truth," and she spoke it quite well. If every Democrat could see her in a small room like this, any hesitation about her charisma would disappear. Question is - can she translate that to big venues and TV?

Apr 20, 2019, 8:30 PM

I'm pretty sure we wouldn't be sitting around saying "oh Hitler, should we impeach him or leave him in place, trying to impeach him will only make him stronger." And I know that Trump is not Hitler - he's worse because he's not some monster from history, he's the president* of our country now, and we can do something about that. Or not. I don't get the argument for not.

Apr 21, 2019, 8:01 AM

It's a beautiful Easter morning at Mar-A-Lago - perfect for tweeting out some demented lies, knocking a ball into a hole, ignoring the wife and child, proclaiming my innocence to the millions who've never read 448 pages of anything, and ordering takeout from Orchids of Asia.

Apr 23, 2019, 12:20 PM

Only in America could you have 44 out of 45 presidents be white males and when someone says Hey why not try a woman, the establishment cries, "stop with the identity politics!" America has practiced identity politics since the first slave arrived in shackles. Now that a woman or a minority member might win, it's time to "stop?"

Apr 25, 2019, 10:23 AM

Trump: Make America White Again
Pence: Make America Men 4 Men
Biden: Make America 2016 Again
Bernie: Make America 2016 Again But I Win
Beto: Make America Denim Again
Buttigieg: Make America Cute Again
Warren: Make America Fair Again
Harris: Make America Smart Again
Klobuchar: I Eat Salad With A Comb

Apr 26, 2019, 12:33 PM

I'd rather have sex with a chump
Eat fish from the dump
Have a measle or mump
Than four more years of Donald Trump

I'd rather outrun Forrest Gump
Give a camel a hump
Climb Eiffel, then jump
Than four more weeks of Donald Trump

I'd rather eat wasps in a clump
Make love to a frump

Suck gas from the pump
Slap Jared's pale rump
Sit hard on a stump
Than have four more days of Donald Trump

Apr 26, 2019, 5:33 PM

Robert E. Lee thought of himself as a noble human being and a great general. Lincoln agreed, and offered him command of the Union Army. But Lee regarded his allegiance to Virginia more highly than the oath he had taken to his country at West Point. He resigned his commission and turned traitor – or patriot, if you asked him.

Before the war, Lee was a slaveholder, not an especially kind or benevolent one. He passed up multiple chances to free his slaves - and then U.S. Grant freed them for him.

Lee was much lauded for his "healing" actions in the years after the war. Oddly, even though he fought for four years to destroy the United States, nobody really considered putting him in prison. They took it all out on cranky old Jeff Davis and let Lee go on to live out his life as a benevolent college president.

As far as whether he was a great general, he was a brilliant defensive tactician but he blew it at Gettysburg, big time. He knew it and was ashamed of his performance there.

Apr 29, 2019, 9:57 AM

Some of the live oaks along Bayou St. John are so old, they rest their elbows on the ground when no one's looking.

Apr 30, 2019, 11:26 AM

An ugly incident among the crows that use our live oak tree as their gathering spot in the hour before dawn and at dusk. Incredible squawking and squabbling at 4 am. Around 7, I spied a crow in our street, unable to fly, hopping from one curb to the other, croaking forlornly.

I tried to tempt him into my gate so at least he would be out of traffic, but no dice. When I came out again a bit later, my intrepid neighbor Mari had taken up the challenge. Mari is a friend to all creatures great and small. She knew the phone number of the French Quarter's Bird Lady, who was thrilled to hear of a crow in need. Bird Lady rushed over from her street with a towel and a small cage. The crow put up no resistance. Bird Lady was delighted, since she already has one crow in her backyard rescue/rehab center and now it will have a friend.

May 1, 2019, 5:13 AM

Trump has just tweeted 38 times in 14 minutes but don't worry, that's just the coke talking.

May 2, 2019, 6:42 AM

GOT is an abbreviation for people who don't have time to say the full title of "Game of Thrones," the 68-hour TV series they are watching.

May 8, 2019, 11:44 AM

The Mueller Report exonerates Trump so *totally* and *completely* that Trump has invoked executive privilege to make sure nobody ever gets to read it. He is doing this for us. Our heads could not take that much exoneration; they would explode.

May 13, 2019, 7:55 AM

I loved the part where Will and Kate went to visit Baby Archie and Kate said Meghan was just common American trash and Meghan said Kate's baby is ugly and would be bald as its father soon and Harry took a swing at Will and Will said Harry was the red-headed horseman's son not even a real prince and the baby threw up on its mother and the Queen came in and told them all to just SHUT UP or she would have them beheaded. Life as a royal is not all corgis and cream.

May 15, 2019, 7:27 AM

Under Alabama law, you can now serve more jail time for being a doctor who helps the victim of a rape by performing an abortion than you will serve for being the rapist.

May 17, 2019, 9:42 AM

The only time I've ever seen a stranger reading one of my books was on an airplane. She made it about five pages, fell asleep, and slept soundly the rest of the way to the destination. Wave if you are still awake.

May 17, 2019, 4:51 PM

Trump's new immigration law says immigrants have to learn English, which seems like an awfully roundabout way to get Melania deported.

May 27, 2019, 7:08 AM

The next time you get a burning urge to climb Everest, like the 10 people who've died so far this season, send me a check for $100,000 and I will send you a picture of yourself on the summit that *nobody* will be able to distinguish from the real thing.

May 29, 2019, 6:33 PM

Breaking: Mueller clarifies. "When I said Trump is NOT NOT guilty, I did not mean to imply he is NOT NOT NOT NOT guilty. Obstruction of justice may NOT be the thing he is NOT guiltiest of, but then again, also. The not-notness of his guiltitude may establish his guilt. Or not."

Jun 4, 2019, 1:53 PM

The Continuing Adventures of Elizabeth and Philip

P: Well? How'd it go?
E: Perfectly beastly.
P: Worse than last time?
E: The same. He brags about crowd sizes. Doesn't seem to realize I read the MI5 reports, there were fifteen people at his inauguration and five of them were his children.
P: And the wife?
E: *sigh* Poor girl. Lights on, nobody home.
P: What did you give them as a gift?
E: A book.

(Pause, they collapse in merriment)

Jun 7, 2019, 9:13 AM

When the last guest left, Charles and Camilla
Had a hearty laugh over Godzilla
Whose First Lady, Melania
Dressed to look like Diania,
"Good taste?" they sniffed. "Not a scintilla."

Jun 11, 2019, 3:17 PM

Brain Surgery Without Anesthesia 48%
Trump 42%

One-Legged Mouth-Foaming Dog 49%
Trump 41%

Reconstituted Freeze-Dried Hitler 49%
Trump 42%

Stubbing Toe Hard On Sharp Post 50%
Trump 41%

Chlorine Gas Leak 49%
Trump 41%

Jun 17, 2019, 6:50 AM
Trump to Stephanopolous: "They do say Abraham Lincoln was treated really badly. I must say that's the one. If you can believe it, Abraham Lincoln was treated supposedly very badly. But nobody's been treated badly like me." Mr. Booth? Paging Mr. Booth.

Jun 17, 2019, 7:15 AM
I wish Americans cared about saving their country as much as the 2,000,000 citizens of Hong Kong currently in the streets. We have more reasons to march than they do. Trump could be gone next week if we cared that much.

Jun 21, 2019, 7:19 PM
Sometimes I find myself wondering, "what is my purpose in life?" And then I remember: "To outlive Donald Trump."

Jun 23, 2019 ·7:56 PM

Jimmy Carter 1976: "I'll never lie to you"
Donald Trump 2019: "I'll always lie to you"

Jun 25, 2019 9:38 PM
Some nights, New Orleans is too damn metaphorical. Tonight it's a shooting in the Desire neighborhood, at the intersection of Piety and Humanity Streets.

Jun 27, 2019 12:21 PM

I predict Bernie and Joe will get into a big wrestling match over which was better, the Victrola or the Gramophone. And then Kamala Harris will win the debate.

Jul 3, 2019 9:49 AM

The First Lady, who's also First Daughter,
Lately has been seen more than she oughter,
Who, in floppity sleeves,
Always underachieves -
She's a hairdo without imprimatur

Jul 3, 2019 8:38 PM

T: I want them to goose-step
G: Sir, goose-stepping is not a skill we train for
T: I don't care, they can learn
G: Sir, I don't think we have time to -
T: And I want them to say "Sieg Heil"
G: Sir, we don't teach them German
T: It's just two words

Jul 4, 2019 10:02 AM

Here's a good question for the Census: "Did you become a citizen when your husband was elected president of the United States?"

Alternate Census Questions:
1. Does your name end in a vowel? (If unsure, mark "R")
2. Have you ever used a Western Union?
3. Would you rather have tacos al carbon or Chick-Fil-A?
4. Do you or have you ever a/ cut grass b/ cleaned house?
5. Who is better, Selena Gomez or Britney?

Jul 5, 2019 6:50 AM

The only news out of Trump's Firecracker Rally last night was this choice passage from his speech, spotted by DementiaWatch:

"The Continental Army suffered a bitter winter of Valley Forge, found glory across the waters of the Delaware and seized victory from Cornwallis of Yorktown. Our army manned the air, it ranned the ramparts, it took over the airports, it did everything it had to do. And at Fort McHendry, under 'the rockets' red glare,' it had nothing but victory."

Jul 5, 2019 5:04 PM

Okay I am just SICK of all you people criticizing Trump! Let's get real!!! How the hell was he supposed to know there weren't airports in 1775 if his TELEPROMPTER WENT OUT!!! How would ANYBODY know a thing like that? People please!

Jul 9, 2019 4:40 PM

Trump says he will no longer work with the British diplomat who said he is "inept." The Brits are now looking for a diplomat who will say he is "ept." The eptliest. Nobody ever had more ept.

Jul 10, 2019 7:48 AM

The British ambassador to the United States has now been fired for calling Trump "inept" and "incompetent."

Help Wanted: One blind, deaf ambassador, any age or gender, prefer candidates with memory loss and a tendency to keep quiet about the obvious.

Jul 11, 2019 3:27 PM

I can't wait till they get those Amazon delivery drones up and running, so I can just go out and shoot down whatever I want. "Look Maw, a flat-screen TV!" Ka-blam!

Jul 13, 2019 5:39 PM

Personally I am going to wait for the animated reimagining of the live-action reimagining of the animated film "The Lion King."

Jul 14, 2019 11:46 AM

Hey Trumpo, we'll discuss sending American-born Congresswomen back to where they came from as soon as your nudie-model fake-visa fake-kidney fake wife goes back to Slovenia.

Jul 15, 2019 10:17 AM

It's not Barron Trump's fault he's an anchor baby.

Jul 20, 2019 9:15 AM

Buzz Aldrin has described his weeks-long, tortuous dance with Neil Armstrong over the question of who would be first to step on the moon. Neil thought his position as commander made it obvious he should be first. Buzz wasn't happy about that. Among other reasons, he would actually have to move out of the way to give Neil access to the door.

Neil was commander. So Neil won that fight.

Buzz has always said only (mostly) good things about Neil, but I have to think he was delighted that when Neil's big moment came, he blew his line. Neil had pondered what to say, and carefully prepared. He tried to say "That's one small step for a man...."

What he actually said was, "That's one small step for man, one giant leap for mankind." Which makes no sense at all.

I love the fact that the very first thing our species did after stepping off our home planet for the first time was to screw up the line and say something nonsensical. It's so ... human.

Aug 2, 2019 2:20 PM

"Trump Eulogies" is trending in Twitter. It's fun and free to write your own!

"A lot of people have come to me and said, "Sir" - big guys with tears in their eyes, they say "Sir, if I ever die, I want you to be the one to say my eulogy," and then they will die right there in front of me, and I stop whatever I'm doing and say it for them."

Aug 3, 2019 11:05 AM

I'll never forget how the illegal immigrant Pilgrims stepped off the *Mayflower* and the natives took away their children and locked them in cages oh wait, no, that is us.

Aug 6, 2019 8:39 AM

Trump will seek to console in El Paso
And in Dayton, because he got lassoed
Into acting the part
Of a man with a heart
I think you know what rhyme will go here

Aug 16, 2019 7:58 AM

Greenland seems cool to the idea of being bought by Trump. Even changing the name to Greedland didn't make a difference. So, up yours Greenland losers! Eat your reindeer hamberder or whatever you eat! Trump has plenty of non-shithole countries he can buy!

For instance he can buy California and sell it to New York. He can buy Russia and sell it to Sarah Palin. He can buy Slovenia and change its name to Melanie, or whatever. He can buy Italy and put a dollar tax on each pizza. He can buy Australia and have it towed to the correct hemisphere.

He can buy Saudi Arabia and - wait, no, sorry, he can't buy Saudi Arabia.

But ... he can buy France and eat all the fries. He can buy Germany and remodel Berchtesgaden into a summer White House anyone would be proud of. He can buy Argentina and stand on a balcony with his arms raised and he can sing sing sing until everyone in the world knows the beauty of his voice.

Aug 22, 2019 3:18 PM

Hello World,

I have decided to buy England. They have that great marmalade. Their palace guards have tall fuzzy hats. They have Rolls-Royce. I will pay exactly $1000.00 cash American for England. I have already sent the money to the Queen via Venmo. If she does not like it, we will rain fire and fury over England like nothing you've ever seen before. England does not have one of these nasty women presidents who will mock me. My idea is not "absurd,"it is "asurb." Boris England has great hair. Anyone who is a Jew is disloyal to Israel. Remember Toledo. Remember Bowling Greenland. Give me England NOW or I kill the Corgi puppy.

Aug 30, 2019 7:24 PM
Trump fired his secretary because she told reporters she has a better relationship with Trump than his daughters, and he hates to pose with Tiffany because he thinks she's fat.

Aug 31, 2019 6:25 PM
Every time I hear the words "active shooter" I think of a video game - bam bam nobody gets hurt, start a new game! But this is not a game. Stop calling them "active shooters." They're white nationalist murderers. Call them what they are.

Aug 31, 2019 8:49 PM
Imagine being such a hideous person that you have to force everyone around you to sign Non-Disclosure Agreements promising they won't tell anyone what a hideous person you are.
Imagine having to take to Twitter to tell your daughter that, contrary to published reports, you do love her.

Sep 1, 2019 10:40 AM
Twenty-six people were gunned down in Odessa, Texas, and there's a deadly hurricane barreling toward our coast, but Private Hairplug skipped out of a trip to Poland to commemorate the start of WWII so he could focus on insulting the actress Debra Messing.
One weird phenomenon of our time is the post-mass-shooting police press conference, underway now in Odessa, in which the law enforcement people preen and congratulate each other and issue thoughts and prayers and thanks and thanks and thanks to each other,

as if they have all just won the Oscar. They proclaim their own heroism and thank each other for it. The politicians dress up as law--enforcement officers for the occasion - the governor wears a black shirt with a big gold star. They say they won't name the gunman because they don't want him to have notoriety, but these men exult in the glow of the cameras and the chance to strut before the nation. I don't know what the answer is, but this spectacle is macabre.

Sep 9, 2019 7:49 PM

Strong men keep coming up to me, big strong men who never cry, and they have tears in their eyes when they thank me for all I've done in Alabama since the hurricane. Sir, they say, thank you for saving us, please save us some more Sir, we are White and We Love You! And I pull out my Sharpie and I sign their arm, right above their tattoo, and they never wash their arm again because I am Sir, and they love me!

Sep 9, 2019 5:04 PM

Todd and Sarah Palin had the perfect marriage. They taught us all how to love. How to run up a huge charge at Neiman-Marcus. How to herd the whole family into the limo after the drunken fistfight. A love like theirs will not soon come this way again. But now it's dead as a turkey in a beheading machine. Thoughts and prayers for Todd and Sarah, and their children Tugg, Trick, Thudd, Thugg and Howanda!

Sep 10, 2020 9:40 AM

What is the word for that moment when the rats fleeing the sinking ship stop to rearrange the deck chairs while the captain backs the Titanic up to make another run at the iceberg?

Sep 11, 2019 8:06 AM

Clear September mornings still make me nervous. I was sitting at my desk in the East Village writing an email when the first plane flew over our building. It was too low and loud over Fifth Avenue. I started counting One one thousand two one thousand. At five came the boom. A little tremble in the floor. I grabbed the remote and there it was live from the local weather chopper, the wounded building with the airplane-shaped scar pouring smoke.

I'm still searching for meaning in that day. But I never forget that little tremble through the soles of my feet on the floor.

Sep 14, 2019 3:15 AM

Eudora Welty told me she spent her first thirty years or so feeling homely. I said it was ironic that she turned out to be the great beauty of her time. Her grin was a little wicked. "I came to that realization much later in life," she said.

Sep 16, 2019 12:14 PM

Trump hates more than half the people in this country and the feeling is increasingly mutual.

Sep 19, 2019 11:23 PM

Giuliani confirms Trump offered a bribe (our money) to a foreign leader in exchange for investigating his political rival. But Hillary's emails.

Sep 20, 2019 2:01 PM

If you conspired with Russia to get yourself elected and got away with it, of course you will do it again, in Ukraine, and everywhere, all around the world. Every chance you get.

We have never had a president* who worked so blatantly and obviously to damage the United States. He has no hesitation to extort a foreign government or two to re-install himself.

Hello, Nancy? Do it now. Do it today. Impeach this Chickenfucker.

Sep 24, 2019 3:53 PM

Nancy. nicely positioned as the last Democrat in America to call for impeachment, will reverse herself a few minutes from now.

Do the Republicans really want to run this guy for a second term? Really?

I've been pretty miserable for three years but I'm going to enjoy the hell out of the Fall of Trump. I am dogpaddling happily in an Olympic-sized swimming pool filled with his cholesterol-rich tears. Smells like Big Macs.

Sep 27, 2019 4:10 PM

Stop telling me Trump is going to ride over the Great Pumpkin Ukrainian Extortion Call and this crime will somehow help him.

He is not a wizard. He is the least popular president* in history and if Democrats are going Ho Hum when he confesses to extortion and collusion on live TV, he may have made you as cynical as he is.

This is the most serious presidential* crime in American history and Trump says "yep you betcha I did it" and some Dems go "there goes that crazy Trump again."

Donald J. Trump @realDonaldTrump

To show you how dishonest the LameStream Media is, I used the word Liddle', not Liddle, in discribing Corrupt Congressman Liddle' Adam Schiff. Low ratings @CNN purposely took the hyphen out and said I spelled the word little wrong. A small but never ending situation with CNN!

6:02 AM · Sep 27, 2019

♡ 79.4K   ♥ 78.5K people are Tweeting about this

Sep 27, 2019 7:50 PM

Impeach me, my sweet impeachable you
Replace me, ultra-replaceable you
One look at you brings out the Nazi in me
It's one of the things that you did not see in me
I love all the arms we sold to Ukraine
Above all, I know it's cold in Ukraine
Don't be a titty baby
Come to Putin, come to Putin do
My sweet impeachable you

Sep 27, 2019 10:09 PM

My fellow Americans,
Let us impeach him by the pussy.
Let us move upon him like a bitch.
If it's what you say, I love it. Especially later in the fall.
Very bad people on one side.

Donald J. Trump @realDonaldTrump · 11h ⌄
As the President of the United States, I have an absolute right, perhaps even a duty, to investigate, or have investigated, CORRUPTION, and that would include asking, or suggesting, other Countries to help us out!

💬 43.5K   🔁 32K   ♡ 132.8K   ⬆

markchildress   ⌄
@markchildress

Replying to @realDonaldTrump

You know all that "absolute right" stuff that Stephen Miller keeps telling you? He's wrong. He's an idiot, and he's wrong. You're an idiot listening to an idiot, and you're wrong. You don't have any "absolute right" to do anything. Except resign. Or die. Either is fine.

9:06 PM · Oct 3, 2019 · Twitter Web App

ılı View Tweet activity

Oct 7, 2019 8:33 AM

This is the tweet that got my account "permanently banned" from Twitter. Some Trumper reported it as a death threat and Twitter rejected my appeals.

Oct 6, 2019 8:17 AM

For three years, Trump committed crime after crime in the Oval Office, hundreds or thousands of crimes. His accomplices stood back and approved and watched him break the laws. Helped him. Aided and abetted and conspired with him to break all the laws.

Every person still working at the White House is complicit. That's why they were hired.

Finally, just weeks ago, T. committed a set of crimes so egregious, so far beyond the pale, so traitorous that even these Quislings realized they had to do something. They knew this call was radioactive. Hot. Ultra-impeachable. It wasn't the first but was somehow worse than the others. They scurried to hide the evidence of The Traitor's treason on the super-secret-server with the other bad calls. They started throwing the furniture (and each other) over the deck rails of the Titanic.

But water is water, and water comes in through a hole. The forward holds are flooded. The watertight doors were not shut in time. The Captain is high and low as a cloud and raging, raging, hurling imprecations against the storm and the half-white whale, Obama, that haunts his waking dreams.

We're all on the ship. The ocean is wide, the night is dark, and there aren't enough lifeboats.

Oct 6, 2019 10:04 AM

Oh for Godsake Joe Biden says Trump is "the most corrupt president in modern history" as if there is some Ur-Trump lurking back in the history books who was worse. There ain't. There weren't. He's the worst ever, the stupidest, most corrupt, most amoral man ever to occupy the White House. His crimes have no equal. I see your Buchanan and raise you two Andrew Johnsons and a William Henry Harrison. None of these men enlisted foreign nations to further their own fortunes! Name me a worse president than Trump! You can't do it!

Biden and Bernie need to move over and make way for the nominee. She knows how to attack and you don't do it by mincing words.

Oct 7, 2019 7:44 AM

Overnight, Trump did the worst thing of his entire presidency. Worse than cheering Nazis. Worse than taking refugee kids from their parents and throwing them in cages. Worse than standing next to Putin at Helsinki and siding with the KGB against the CIA.

When W. Bush kicked over the anthill of the Middle East, the Kurds were our allies. They fought and died alongside our soldiers to overturn Saddam Hussein. They have been our most steadfast supporters ever since, as the USA sought to counter ISIS in the region.

Last night Trump talked to his buddy Erdogan, dictator of Turkey, and made a snap decision to abandon the Kurds. This will please Putin. And ISIS. And dictators everywhere who want to ethnically "cleanse" their countries. Trump's hasty action overnight will probably cause the deaths of tens of thousands of people who trusted us.

Now that he knows he will be impeached, the pace of his crimes will increase. He's desperate and wants to wreck the world on his way out the door. If he can't be an influence for good, he's just fine being an influence for evil.

Oct. 7, 2019 10:48 AM

After Twitter suspended my account, I signed up for a new account under a pseudonym.

Abraham Lincoln @SurrealALincoln · Apr 14   ooo
As you can imagine, it's hurtful to see John Wilkes Booth trending on Twitter. I need to see that like I need a hole in the head! Oh well, I guess Mary and I will try to find a comedy to see tonight, to take our minds off everything. Suggestions welcome!

   ♡ 84   ↻ 212   ♡ 1.2K   ⬆   ꓲꓲꓲ

Oct 8, 2019 11:48 AM

"In my great and unmatched wisdom I hereby declare that my ankle shall be the ruler of Antarctica. My ankle, which I call Thunderbone, will be just and honorable in his governance of this land of ice. This governance shall be supervised by my opposite ankle, which shall be known as Fred."

Oct 10, 2019 9:33 AM

On the day we abandoned the Kurdish fighters to their fate, Melania Trump broke ground for a new tennis court at the White House.

Oct 12, 2019 7:08 AM

Trumpy: A person who gets a sexual thrill from hearing an old man say the word "bullshit" out loud

Oct 12, 2019 4:13 PM

Being a Trump secretary of homeland security must feel like being the world's second oldest living man, and being informed that the world's oldest living man has just died, so you are now number next in line.

Oct 14, 2019 8:29 PM

Wouldn't you know that when it came time for America to get its own Hitler, we would get Stupid Hitler?

Hitler was cunning, not stupid. He outfoxed every opponent in Germany and conquered Europe before anyone stood up to stop him.

This guy is cunning AND stupid. It may be that his stupidity ("let me commit the crime more loudly and publicly in case you missed it the first time") will save us. But it could be that his stupidity ("let me screw up every alliance we have and turn the whole world against us") will seal our doom.

Oct 14, 2019 6:05 PM

Trump is upset that he might not get "due process." I will share his message with Jamal Khashoggi.

Oct 15, 2019 8:12 AM

Just off the phone with World Leader-1. My call was perfect in every way. Nobody can believe how congenial I was. I was so goddamn congenial you might want to puke. Strong men come up to me with tears in their eyes and say Sir, I have NEVER seen you so congenial! They weep and fall to their knees. Everybody knows the price of American aid is more dirt on Joe Biden. Send dirt! I give the best aid for good dirt! Don't you brang me no bad dirt! Perfect call. Perfect! 100%!!!

Oct 16, 2019 7:41 AM

No one asked for my impressions of last night's endless Democratic debate, so here they are:

Elizabeth Warren, now in front, seemed taken aback to receive most of the incoming fire. She parried well, but most of the damage inflicted last night was on her.

Kamala Harris had several of the best moments of the night, but everyone seems to have written her off for some reason I can't quite fathom.

Amy Klobuchar made her strongest impression yet. On a ticket with Warren or Harris she would be formidable.

Pete Buttigieg has appointed himself Young Biden and went after Warren with a preview of his cerebral-yet-unforgiving attack style.

Bernie Sanders looked a lot more robust than Joe Biden. One of his best performances.

Joe Biden didn't talk much, but did give a strong defense of being an old white guy with experience.

Cory Booker launched his campaign for VP, defending Biden from Trump and singing "Kumbaya" at regular intervals.

Julian Castro played nice to avoid the bad press he took for attacking Biden last time. He faded into the woodwork.

Beto kept doing that thing where he says what everybody else says, but makes it sound more pious, self-serving, and preachy.

Andrew Yang just doesn't do it for me, don't know why. Might be an interesting Sec of Commerce.

Tulsi Gabbard makes me crazy. She carries water for Putin and Trump. Who supports her?

Tom Billionaire, just go away. Go buy a large island and be president of that.

Oct 17, 2019 9:04 AM

We:

1. abandoned ally A
2. stood by watching ally B slaughter ally A

3. got attacked, ourselves, by ally B
4. bombed our air base, the one we abandoned four days before
5. rushed in to force surrender of ally A to ally B
6. bragged about solving the crisis in Syria
7. gave Syria to Russia

Oct 18, 2019 6:47 AM

The cease-fire has ceased
The bombs fall again:
The Kurds are no(w) angels
The Turks are our friends

A great day for freedom
A great day for us
A great day to throw the Kurds
Under the bus

The Tweeter is tweeting
He made a great deal
He's found an entirely
New way to steal:

Just choose your own hotel
Invite all your friends,
Taxpayers will pay
The means justify ends

Are you feeling hopeless?
More us's than thems
But the Electoral College
Could do that again

Oct 20, 2019 5:34 PM
    I can have the G-1 summit at my apartment if it is Macron, or the
G-2 if it is Macron and Trudeau.

Oct 21, 2019 8:31 AM

When I was about seven years old, my mother allowed my brother and I to have a sleepover at some neighbors' we didn't know very well. About 1 a.m. my brother and I woke up and decided we couldn't stand the smell in that house. I can't put my finger on it but I can still smell it all these years later. Unfamiliar cleaning products? It was worse than that. Something rotten, a heavy hint of untended diapers (this was years before Pampers)?

We woke up the neighbor lady and made her call our mom and dad who came and got us and took us home where everything smelled fine.

That's how I imagine it would be to spend a night at a Trump hotel.

Oct 21, 2019 2:41 PM

Found: the "Phony" Emoluments Clause to the Constitution

"No Dictator or President of the United States shall accept any Emoluments from any King, Prince, or Foreign State, unless that President* be very rich upon taking office; or unless he has played a principal role in a highly-rated Reality Television Program before taking office; or unless he shall have extraordinarily diminutive Hands; or unless his Golf Club offers a series of Well-Appointed Bungalows holding 50 to 75 persons in each Bungalow; or, unless said King or Prince should have a good connection with the Maserati Dealer, and can Obtain a Great Discount from Said Dealer for the President* forthwith."

Oct 22, 2019 8:47 AM

Trump took an oath to defend and protect the Constitution. Calling the Emoluments Clause "phony" is, in itself, another impeachable offense.

Oct 24, 2019 9:00 PM

If Trump bursts from the residence tomorrow, bleeding from one nostril and both eyes, cavorting and capering before the cameras in a sagging Depends adult undergarment while flinging handsful of

M&Ms at the Secret Service men chasing him, screaming "Witch hunt! Witch hunt! My safe word is Hillary! Hilllllaaaaarrrrryyyyyy!" Republicans will say "he's really fighting back now!"

Oct 25, 2019 10:47 PM

Listening to Obama's eulogy for Elijah Cummings, I was pondering the challenge facing Trump's eventual eulogist, whenever that sad day might come.

"He had the greatest crowds ever to witness any inauguration in history, or if not, he truly believed that he did, and sought to make everyone share in his vision."

"His hands were of a size most would consider perfectly normal."

"His love for his daughter Ivanka was well-documented and quite extraordinary."

"He was, indeed, at the end of the day, when all is said and done, when the final page is turned, one of the presidents America has ever had."

"His hair was his own, and worked much harder than other peoples' hair to do the job it was asked to do."

Oct 25, 2019 7:28 PM

Man did I have a perfect phone call today. It was so, so perfect. It was the Mt Olympus of phone calls. It was the Michael Phelps of phone calls. If a phone call could be Grace Kelly in "Rear Window," this would be that call. Perfect. Without a single flaw. People came up to me, big strong guys came up to me with tears in their eyes, and they said "Sir, excuse me Sir, we are weeping because we have never witnessed a phone call of such perfection.'"

Oct 27, 2019 7:18 PM

Trump is going to the World Series tonight to see if the Astros have any dirt on Joe Biden.

Oct 28, 2019 11:58 AM

I am delighted to think that being booed at the World Series bothers Trump so much he hasn't even been able to bring himself to tweet about it.

Don Junior keeps desperately tweeting that Pawpaw should wear the booing as a badge of honor.

You know Pawpaw won't be able to restrain himself for long:

"They weren't booing, they were reminding me it's Halloween"

"No president* has ever gotten a reception like that! The Bezos Washington Post says 100 decibels! A record!"

"Baseball is a stupid washed-up game for losers so I left after the 7th"

Oct 29, 2019 2:28 AM

The first President to warn about global warming was Lyndon Johnson in a speech in 1965. So we've only had 54 years to do something about it.

Oct 30, 2019 2:10 PM

"I could stand in the middle of Fifth Avenue and shoot someone," Trump said.

Jeffrey Epstein died at the Metropolitan Correctional Center, roughly two miles south of Fifth Avenue. That's all I'm saying.

Nov 1, 2019 2:45 PM

Trump joked that his wife Melanie wouldn't cry if he got shot. Heck no, she'd be busy polishing her fingerprints off the pistol. "Boris? It's Natasha. Bring in me from the cold."

Nov 3, 2019 4:05 PM

The Trump administration is a worldwide mafia shakedown operation in which the innocent shopkeeper nations of the world are extorted and threatened by the bully chieftain   into helping him exterminate his enemies. Or is it just me?

Nov 7, 2019 5:29 AM

Trump says if he's removed we'll suffer a depression like nobody's ever seen before. Don't know about you, but for me the word "impeachment" is the ultimate anti-depressant.

Nov 9, 2019 7:55 AM

In 1974 Richard Nixon went to the last place in America where he believed he would be cheered by the public. That was the Mississippi Coliseum in Jackson. As a high school band student we were bused in and encouraged to cheer for him. Against the wishes of our band director, Howard Cohen. This episode was a chapter of my novel "One Mississippi" that I cut before publication.

Now, fresh off his World Series Halloween boo-fest, here comes Donald Trump to the last place in America where he believes he will be cheered. Tuscaloosa. Bama-LSU game day. Let's hope like hell that the 40 pct good folks of Alabama boo loud enough to be heard over all the morons who didn't even go to school there.
[The booing was just audible.]

Nov 11, 2019 5:40 AM

"Anonymous" says a group of Trump's top advisors considered resigning en masse "to save the country" from Trump. Then what? I guess they decided nope, we're good, no need to save the country. Let's continue to cover our own asses and try to quietly undermine him from the inside. "Profiles in (Occasional, Tentative) Courage (In Retrospect, Anyway)"

Nov 11, 2019 4:09 PM

At the risk of sounding bitter
About the Great Counterfeiter
He's a nasty little twitter
He's a serial emitter

He's a bald red-faced hairsplitter
He's a porno star remitter
I wish he would be a quitter
Instead of an evil transmitter
A vapid switch-hitter
A spume, spew, and spitter
But he's not.
But I'm not bitter.

Nov 18, 2019 12:23 PM

He can only offer written answers because his dementia, idiocy, and rage would lead to inevitable catastrophe if he were to take the stand. Let this sink in. The "leader of the free world" cannot answer questions under oath.

Nov 20, 2019 4:30 PM

I hereby deny that I have denied my previous denial. Not only do I deny it, I deny saying to you what I am saying to you right now. I am not even talking to you except to deny I have ever failed to deny all my earlier denials.

Nov 22, 2019 7:50 PM

I had just turned six. I loved JFK because he played with his kids under the desk in the Oval Office. I wished for a blindingly handsome dad who would ever play with me. We were at recess when word swept the playground: Kennedy got shot in the head. Most kids didn't know who Kennedy was but I was in love with him, so I cried. The teacher called us in and said the President was dead so we should all go home. All our mothers were home to receive us without notice. My mother sat us in front of the TV and told us to watch. I lay awake that night worrying about Caroline who was also six and lost her daddy. Nothing has ever been quite right in the United States since that day.

Nov 24, 2019 6:31 AM

Starbucks 6 am. Like any decent human being, I want a cup of coffee. And I will have it, eventually, as soon as the lady in front of me gets her Grande Double Shot Mocha Cloud Foam Cold Brewed Chocolate Macchiato Caramel Salted Cookie Crunch Cocoa Ribbon Frappuccino.

Dec 3, 2019 5:52 PM

My favorite candidate, Kamala Harris, quit the race today. So I hate everybody. I thought she was our best standard-bearer. I'm sorry that our nominee will probably be white. I really thought a black woman nominee made the most effective contrast/opponent for Trump. But politics is not just about getting votes or getting poll numbers, it's about money. And Harris quit because she says she can't compete with billionaires.

Dec 4, 2019 7:46 AM

Republicans prefer Putin to Hillary. They prefer Putin to any Democrat. We can't win unless we admit that. They would rather Russians take over our country than black people or Latinos or Asians or gay people or women.

We must proceed with impeachment. His followers will not be convinced. They must be defeated. Impeaching him will help us remove him in November, if the Senate fails to act.

Dec 4, 2019 8:46 AM

I sat next to a rich older lady in a doctor's waiting room yesterday. She had an interminable cellphone conversation with a friend, so that we all got to listen to her end of it. She started by commiserating with our poor First Lady, "easily the most elegant First Lady we've ever had," and purred into the phone how sad it is that so many people hate her.

Then she observed that the First Lady's son Barron is "incredibly good looking" and that people should be more fair to Trump. Then they moved to Ivanka and said she is "naturally just gorgeous," which was another reason people should be nicer to Trump. Then she mentioned "the other daughter" who "doesn't have much to do with them" and "isn't as pretty as the others."

I was giving her the biggest possible stinkeye, but the lady kept going. "They just want to let anybody come into this country, black brown gay or whatever."

I coughed in a way that sounded like "hey lady shut up now." She ignored me.

She purred and hummed. Her friend on the other end commiserated with the idea that it's sad people are so hateful to the First Family since they are all so good-looking.

I did not say a word. I sat there with my jaw clamped. For this, I want the fucking Nobel Peace Prize and I want it now.

Dec 13, 2019 9:14 AM

On the bright side: the House Judiciary Committee has approved two articles of impeachment against Trump. He will be impeached. There will be a trial. Don't tell me not to be happy about this. Justice is slow but she is being served.

Dec 18, 2019 9:46 AM

Time to drive this whale up on the beach
Time to wash out our ears with the bleach
Time for mermaids to sing, each to each
Time to pull off the bloodsucking leech
I don't need you to make me a speech
I don't need you to teach, or unteach
I don't want you to fear overreach
I just want you to vote to impeach.

Dec 25, 2019 6:58 AM

I hate to break the news to all my snowflake friends - but we have been fed a LINE OF MALARKEY about Rudolph.

Just listen to the lyrics. The dude is a bullying victim, sure, so he deserves a big reversal by the end. He deserves to have all the reindeer (suddenly) love him. He deserves to be shouted out, by them, with glee. But what exactly did he do to earn these kudos?

A glowing nose is a genetic condition. It is nature, not nurture. He did nothing to earn it. No free will was involved, no expertise, no training. Rudolph did NOT make a choice. If his leg turned yellow and started beeping, would anyone get excited? Would they award him an honorary degree if his ears turned blue and gave off an intoxicating scent of frangipani?

It's like everyone shouting out with glee because you happen to have been born with one green eye and one brown eye.

And then - Rudolph's freakish nose lights up SO BRIGHT that he enables gift-delivery to proceed around the globe - okay just STOP.

Have you ever been in a really thick fog? Trying to drive and you turn the headlights on bright? What happens? You're blinded. You can't see a thing. A bright light in a fog is COMPLETELY USELESS as a navigational aid.

So, who stands to benefit from the propagation of this ridiculous myth? In whose interest is it to present Rudolph as a shining beacon of hope, clarity, and a flood of retail goods?

There's a clue embedded in the lyrics. What color is his nose? Is it red-white-and-blue, the color of America and post-revolutionary France? Oh heck no. It's red. Red as Red Square. Red as the sunburn of Putin riding shirtless on a horse. This is a well-known fact. Everybody is saying it. I have heard people saying it, I am not saying it but a lot of people are. I don't know all the questions, but I know all the antlers.

Dec 29, 2019 6:19 PM

Why do the storm troopers in "Star Wars" bother to wear that white plastic armor? You can kill any one of them with one shot from any weapon. The rebels, on the other hand, have never worn armor and they are all still fine after 42 years of "Star Wars" movies.

Dec 30, 2019 7:25 AM

Trump's New Year resolutions:

1. Me me me

2. Bigger hands
3. Patch things up with Stormy, or
4. 2nd date with Ivanka
5. Sock rocket
6. Diet Coke
7. Golf
8. Twitter
9. Rally
10. Disown "sons"

2020

Jan 2, 2020 10:05 AM

If I was pope and I was 83 and I was working a pope-on-a-rope-line and some woman seized my arm and almost knocked me down, I would give her more than a couple of smacks on the wrist - I would put the massive Popehold on her and take her DOWN!!! Go for it, Francis – people need to realize they can't just MESS with no pope!

Shouldn't Pope Frank have better security? Hello Vatican cops? Does the name John Paul II ring a bell?

Jan 7, 2020 8:44 AM

Americans go around like "why do these other countries want to rule the world" but if you think about it the only country that goes around acting like they rule the world is America.

Jan 7, 2020 4:46 PM

Iran attacked us because we attacked them because they attacked us because we attacked them because they attacked us because their fathers attacked our fathers because our fathers attacked their fathers because their grandfathers attacked our grandfathers because our grandfathers attacked their grandfathers CAN I STOP NOW?

Jan 17, 2020 5:43 PM

Trump was supposed to be celebrating the LSU football team but of course that meant celebrating himself. He said there have been "a lot of presidents — some good, some not so good."

"But you've got a good one now," he went on, "even though they are trying to impeach the son of a bitch."

Don't look at me! That's what he said!

He will not be convicted. His henchmen are conspiring with all their might to fix the result. But he will always, always be the impeached man. His anguished tweets make me happy.

Jan 20, 2020 7:09 AM

Trump: "Farmers have a lot of guts. Come on, there's not one person that dislikes their children because they're brats? Because they're spoiled, rotten brats? Ok, well that's a pretty good group of people. That's the farmers for you."

On Eric! On Junior! Ivanka and Tiffany! Daddy's high, he's been up all night, he's projecting again....

Jan 20, 2020 9:04 AM

Trump is a stable genius because everything that comes out is horseshit.

Jan 21, 2020 7:34 PM

There is something satisfying about forcing all 100 of the Senators to give up their phones and sit in the chamber and listen to the case being made by the House impeachment managers. We the people, the Democrats, forced them to do this. Right now Hakeem Jeffries is speaking for us.

The senators can't talk to each other, they can't read a book. They can doze off but that's about the only way out of hearing Trump's crimes described in detail. It's boring but it's also compelling.

Even the viewers of Fox are seeing this, and hearing every word. Trump won't be removed in this trial but this is helping lead to his destruction.

Jan 22, 2020 8:28 AM

Every eighty-eight seconds I tweet
I can even send tweets with my feet

I think it, I tweet it
I tweet it, I eat it
I eat with my feet while I tweet!

Jan 24, 2020 8:26 AM

If you were watching last night, you saw Adam Schiff give a quiet and powerful closing argument in the impeachment trial.

His basic message was: you Senators know you cannot depend on this president* to choose the country's interest over his own. And this is why you must remove him. I doubt it made much difference to those with their minds already made up.

Feb 2, 2020 7:32 PM

I could dance like Miss Jennifer Lopez and Shakira at the Super Bowl if I practiced 10 minutes every day. I also believe my dog is the reincarnation of the comic actor Don Knotts. Also, I don't have a dog.

Feb 4, 2020 9:56 PM

Nancy Pelosi sure as hell represented me when she ripped those pieces of paper in two and threw them down on the desk. With that simple, inelegant gesture, she represented the majority of Americans who impeached the man, and want him gone, not giving pompous blasts of hot air in the Capitol.

She took his victory lap away from him by simply tearing some papers in two. That's leadership.

Feb 5, 2020 1:28 PM

Good for Mitt Romney. The only Republican who will vote to convict. The first ever to vote to remove a president* of his own party. Good for Mitt.

Feb 7, 2020 4:33 PM

Trump just fired a Purple Heart recipient and had him perp--walked out of the White House for the crime of testifying under oath after a Congressional subpoena. Don would have done the escorting himself except his bone spurs were aching.

Feb 10, 2020 1:06 PM

Trump's new budget: Adderall, burnt steaks, hamberders, Sharpies, guns, tacky tasteless gifts for fellow autocrats, and $50bn in new funding for Obama Erasure.

All you have to do to hit the high point in your Gallup poll is to get impeached and fake-acquitted by your lackeys. America is more gullible than ever.

Feb 11, 2020 7:43 PM

When you think back to *Citizens United* and *Shelby County vs. US*, the only logical outcome is billionaire vs. billionaire in the race for president.

If money is free speech, and voter suppression is fine, then only billionaires will be able to afford enough speech and the suppression of their opponent's votes. The speech of the billionaires will drown out everybody else.

Feb 19, 2020 9:46 PM

Chuckie Todd: Your closing thoughts?
Bloomberg: Is this live? Can I buy this? Can we destroy these tapes?
Amy: I hate Pete
Pete: I hate Amy
Elizabeth: I will systematically destroy each of you tonight, one by one. None of you will survive. One by one I will take you out. Except Bernie.
Biden: I am the only one here who ever did anything!
Bernie: Like all Vermonters, I have a summer camp.

Feb 24, 2020 3:45 PM

White House sources want us to believe "Trump" was enraged by the idea of putting the infected coronavirus patients on the same plane with the uninfected people, but what he actually said was "my sock rocket is bright shiny blue, plus like I told you I have an overdoth of beeble."

Feb 26, 2020 4:40 PM

Trump was completely flabbergasted to learn that 25,000-69,000 Americans die every year from the influenza. He says that the fact that there are "only" 15 cases of this coronavirus in the US proves that he is doing a good job. How many cases will it take to prove he is doing a bad job?

What a relief that he has chosen to lead the response to this coronavirus Mike Pence, who doesn't believe in science.

Feb 27 , 2020 1:55 PM

I think the Trumpers should keep having their rallies and they should not listen to any stupid liberals who tell them to wash their hands or wear a mask or cover their mouths when they sneeze. "Wash your hands?" What do they think we are, babies? That is liberal propaganda. The liberals are trying to get good Americans to kill the beneficial viruses on their skin with this indiscriminate washing. Don't fall for it! Go to a Trump rally today! Hug and kiss the person next to you! If you see people sneezing or feverish, remember, the coronavirus is not contagious among Republicans. Enjoy the rally!

Feb 28, 2020 8:00 AM

Dow futures down 607. That screaming plummeting sound you're hearing from Wall Street is the sound of all those who pretended you don't need a good competent human being with a functioning brain as president, coming to the sudden realization that you do.

All those old white men on CNBC telling us this panic is overblown are exactly the same people who said exactly the same thing in 2007-08 as the financial system collapsed.

Feb 29, 2020 7:36 AM

Hey Don, it's all a big hoax? Prove it to us! Go to Wuhan, China, and take a long slow stroll around town. I'll wait right here.

Mar 4, 2020 9:10 PM

I always wondered how you could possibly go broke in the casino business, but that was before I heard Trump try to grasp the concept of a double blind clinical trial.

Mar 10, 2020 6:29 PM

Three cases of Covid-19 in the New Orleans area. The mayor just announced cancellation of all public events this weekend, and St. Patrick Day parades. NOLAns freaking out twitterly. The mayor says she'll be talking to French Quarter Fest, Essence and other big festivals ... these festivals are very important to New Orleans' tourist economy.

In the 1918 influenza pandemic, the mayor of Philadelphia refused to cancel a huge Victory parade celebrating the end of World War I, and 200,000 people marched in it. St Louis' mayor shut down the whole city, like Wuhan. Death rate in St. Louis was half that of Philly.

Mar 10, 2020 9:21 PM

Trump has just proved that if you put out enough bull you can turn it into a bear market. Meantime, Joe Biden is doing a fantastic job of not being Donald Trump. Go Joe!

Mar 11, 2020 6:07 PM

I'm not worried about Extreme Social Distancing. They tried that on me for a whole year in the seventh grade and I didn't mind at all.

Mar 12, 2020 7:36 AM

If you didn't get a chance to hear the worst, most counter-productive, most addled, confused and confusing presidential* address in history, please take a moment to watch it.

Stock futures market plunged 1100 points in a few minutes after this "reassuring" emission of babble and lies. The White House and separate federal agencies hurried to issue "clarifications" of the misstatements in the prepared text of the speech - not ad libs.

"Trump" said he was instituting a complete travel ban from China. False - we will continue to admit all red-blooded American virus carriers.

No telling how many who are alive right now will die because of this man. And forty percent of Americans have lost their minds.

Every time some official on TV spends time exclaiming about the emperor's new clothes, thanking him for his brilliant decisions, they are killing people. Use that time to pass vital life-saving information to the American people. Stop stroking Trump when people are dying.

Mar 12, 2020 6:35 PM

The orange king wrote upon his papyrus
"Of an end to this plague, I'm desirous
I've been knocked to my knees
For an innocent sneeze
Don't blame me! This is a Chinese virus"

Mar 15, 2020 5:09 PM

They're going to work all the kinks out of the testing system just about the time the pandemic is so universally widespread that testing won't mean a goddamn thing any more.

Mar 17, 2020 3:42 PM

BREAKING: Vice President Mike Pence suffered a broken nose at today's press conference when Trump stood up abruptly without warning.

Mar 18, 2020 11:27 AM

I am leaning forward. I am leaning in hard. I am expanding my capacity. I am deploying my resources. I am keeping Extreme Social Distance. I am observing Radical Sanitation. I maintain a six-foot Cordon Sanitaire about my person at all moments. I am a ship called Mercy or Comfort. I am a vector. I am a carrier. I am a rock. I am an island. I am a consumer. I am a risk citizen. I am a sponge of infection. I am a beacon of bleach. I am your government, drowning in the bathtub. I am a rich person calling to buy my own ventilator. I am an investor looking for a play. I am leaning in. I am leaning in hard. I am reaching out. I am thanking you for reaching out. I would like to thank all the little people who made this virus possible. It was an honor just to be exposed.

Mar 19, 2020 3:50 PM
I hope everyone will enjoy my recipe for "Quarantine Casserole."

1. Preheat oven to 350.
2. Take everything out of the refrigerator that looks like it is about to go bad, or has only gone a little bit bad
3. Chop it all up and put it in a casserole dish
4. Top with cheese and hot sauce
5. Bake for 30 minutes or until you are tired of baking it.

Mar 21, 2020 7:10 AM
Bad Daddy got mad and yelled at everybody yesterday. Now all the kids are thinking up ways to make him stop being mad. Maybe we could ask nicer questions. Maybe we could tell him how great he is, before he yells at us. Maybe his bad mood is all our fault. Maybe if we were nicer to him, he could stop yelling at us. Why do we always get in his way? After all, he is trying to deal with something that has never happened before, that no one could have predicted. (Except everybody did.)

Mar 22, 2020 8:40 AM
Dr. Trump's Magic Elixir is coming Tuesday! Very excited! Damn the side effects, full speed ahead! Total cure expected by Friday. at latest! Better buy stocks now! I am the greatest! Nothing this bad has ever happened in the history of humanity! This is the worst! I am the best! Step right up, folks! Get your Free Money!

Mar 23, 2020 2:43 PM
One week from now Trump will tire of doctors telling him what to do and will order everybody "Back to Work." You can hear the beat of the drums already.
Economy first! What's a few hundred thousand lives more or less?

Theory: Trump spent what, two days in social isolation with Melanie and his youngest son Whatshisname? And he's ready to call off the entire national anti-pandemic effort just to get the hell out of there.

Mar 30, 2020 9:43 PM

"I could stand in the middle of Fifth Avenue and shoot 100,000-
-200,000 people and wouldn't lose any votes, okay?"

Seven hundred and eighty Americans died today of a virus Trump was still calling a hoax one month ago.

Bodies piling up? Don't look at me, I voted for the lady who put those work emails on her home computer.

April 3, 2020, 7:19 AM

How many people will die because the Trump administration didn't tell the American people to wear masks in public?

Now they seem to be changing their minds and hinting that yes, we probably should wear masks, although they're still dithering.

A mask won't prevent your catching the virus, but will reduce your chance of infecting others - and yourself. If everyone wore masks, the spread will slow down.

We could have been crash-manufacturing cloth masks during these weeks while they dithered, but as Jared Kushner says, a crisis shows the voters who the good managers are.

April 3, 2020 4:35 PM

The new recommendation from CDC, according to Trump, is that you should wear a mask, or not, but he is not going to, but you can if you want, but it won't help, so don't do it, but we recommend that you do, so please don't, he's not going to, so the recommendation is a yes, but also no.

April 3, 2020 7:45 PM

Not since Jonestown have we had so many Americans cheering on a madman while he was busy arranging the circumstances of their deaths.

April 6, 2020 7:31 AM

Today the 10,000th American will die of COVID-19, a pandemic that was preventable only three months ago. Is this what Trump meant when he gave himself a "10 out of 10?"

April 6, 2020 8:51 AM

We all know what's coming next: The first signs of flattening the curve in Italy and Spain will give great cheer to the "reopen America" people (Trump) and they will rush us into a relaxation of the distancing measures and our curve will keep going up and up and up.

Because the truth is, and we all know it: the USA has not come anywhere close to Spain or Italy in their extremely strict observance of distancing/shutdowns. Nationally, our effort is half-assed and half-hearted, at best.

And Fauci will quit or get fired.

And Birx will run out of new scarves and realize Trump is blaming everything on her.

And many Americans will die who did not have to die now, because 52 American senators didn't remove the incompetent oaf when they had the chance.

April 7, 2020 8:19 AM

Woke up this morning, made a cup of coffee. No one ever made a better cup of coffee. No one could ever have expected a cup of coffee to taste that good. It was amazing. I was amazing. I was the only one who made that coffee. Everyone is saying what a great job I did making it. No one has ever even tried to make a cup of coffee - well, I like to call it 'a cup of coffee,' others call it other things - NO one has even tried to make a cup of coffee under these conditions. I was amazed to find out that some people make coffee every day, can you believe that? No, I inherited a bad coffeemaker from the previous tenants. They did not replenish the coffee supply. But the coffee I made, that was like no coffee you have ever seen. I drank it very strongly, very powerfully. It was a nasty, horrid, horrible cup of coffee. Why did you have to ask me that? Who are you with?

April 7, 2020 11:30 AM

Stephanie Grisham is out as press secretary. She's being rushed back to Melania's office to try to save the much-delayed Tennis Pavillion (sic). Can't believe how the silly old virus has delayed this vital project!

You people laugh. But a First Lady without a functioning, completed Tennis Pavillion is like an Empress of France with no cake! Does no one understand the sacrifice and suffering of Melania in this trying time?

April 8, 2020 11:44 AM

Three weeks ago I started learning to sew masks because my friends in Vietnam were scolding me for not wearing one. At that time, the USA had about 1000 cases of Cv-19, and Vietnam had 115. Today, Vietnam has 251 cases. The USA has 400,549.

April 10 2020 8:58 AM

NO ONE knows the pain of being in the middle of a pandemic with sky-high television ratings and everybody on earth IGNORES IT!!!!!

Donald J. Trump ✔
@realDonaldTrump

The Wall Street Journal always "forgets" to mention that the ratings for the White House Press Briefings are "through the roof" (Monday Night Football, Bachelor Finale, according to @nytimes) & is only way for me to escape the Fake News & get my views across. WSJ is Fake News!

2:35 PM · Apr 9, 2020   ⓘ

April 11, 2020 10:48 AM

Questions I would like to ask Trump:

"How many dead Americans would it take for you to drop your rating of yourself from a 10 to a 9?"

"Where is Melanie hiding?"

"Do you realize that those eye-circles make you look like a burnt umber raccoon with dementia?"

April 15, 2020 10:03 AM

The United States has the most cases and most deaths in the world because wc had the worst government response to the pandemic in the world because we have the worst government leader* running the worst-run government in the world. We will not begin to recover before the source of our illness is gone.

What Trump learned from closing it down too late is that we need to open it up too early.

April 16, 2020 5:23 PM

Death very very powerfully death.
Deaths very strongly deaths.
Deaths like no one has ever seen before.
So much dying, you'll get sick of dying.
Death will just wash on through, wash right through in April.
We're so thankful for death.

Very powerfully greatest strongly death anybody's ever seen.
God bless our death.
Land of the death.
Home of the death.

April 17, 2020 4:24 PM

These infect-me people protesting the stay-home orders remind me of the idiots in "Independence Day" dancing atop the skyscraper and shouting welcome to the aliens who were getting ready to blast them into microbits.

Does it seem to you that Republicans are a hell of a lot more eager than Democrats to get the hell away from their homes and families? One month and they're all ready to re-hire the nanny and go hide in the cubicle at work, even at risk of their lives. Must get old sitting around bitching about Obama and commenting on the wisdom of Tucker Carlson.

April 18, 2020 9:25 AM

Mark down May 2 on your calendar. That's 14 days from today the day we'll see a spike in cases in New Orleans because today everybody decided to go out of their houses. Because yesterday Trump sent the secret bat-virus-signal: "Open America Again!"

I have been restricting my grocery run to early Saturday mornings because NO ONE is on the street and NO ONE is in the store.

Today I saw more people on the streets and sidewalks than I've seen since March 12. I didn't see anyone wearing a mask except me and the grocery lady and the delivery guy, who said it was the most people he'd seen outside in a month.

The pandemic must be over! Liberate New Orleans! I think the righties are using Trump's bat-virus signal as an excuse to go out and mingle.
[The spike arrived later in May]

April 21, 2020 7:16 AM

Upon the Occasion of Her Majesty Elizabeth II's Birthday

Happy ninety-fourth birthday, old Queen
What a marvelous queen you have been
It's true you got jewels
Suffered so many fools -
One more, ma'am. Outlive that tangerine!

April 22, 2020 8:18 AM

It's been so long, darlin, since I felt your sweet touch
Hair down to my shoulders, I need you so much
To smell that lime-rosemary shampoo you use
These bangs in my eyes have just left me confused

A haircut -
Tattoo -
A mani, a pedi,
Where can I buy widely-distanced confetti
I need a massage, dear, we'll leave lots of room
Everybody deserves happy endings on Zoom

I need to go bowling, I need to run free
I need a tat of Brian Kemp on my knee
My toenails are longer than they've ever been
The milk in the fridge is older than the Queen

A haircut
Tattoo -
A mani, a pedi,
I look in the mirror, I see Estelle Getty
When the 'Demic is over, we'll all shout hooray
And save up our Charmin for the next rainy day

April 23, 2020 7:54 AM
     You can hate Twitter, and I do, but then Surreal Abe Lincoln gets
retweeted by Martina Navratilova, and life is good!

April 23, 2020 1:04 PM

New Orleans was an early hotspot, of course. Mitigation started earlier here than anywhere but Seattle and New Rochelle. We were blessed with a good Democratic governor and a good Democratic mayor who listen to their health experts. So we are seeing a good result, flattening the curve. For those in places where the peak will come later, I hope you listen to the doctors and not the (R)s.

April 23, 2020 5:28 PM

Doctor Trump says we should either shoot tremendous light inside our bodies to kill the virus, or drink rubbing alcohol or Clorox or maybe inject them into us.

"Supposing we hit the body with tremendous, ultra-violet or just very powerful light? Supposing you brought the light inside the body, either through the skin, or some other way?"

If Fauci would just say "Mr President*, that is the dumbest fucking thing any human being has ever said in my presence," I would swim to South Africa, mine gold and refine it, and hand-cast the medal for a Nobel Prize which I would give to Fauci myself, on my hands and knees.

April 24, 2020 7:38 AM

Got a fever and bad cough last night, but I took three Tide Pods and ate a glow stick. Feeling much better.

April 24, 2020 5:29 PM

It finally happened. Trump finally said something so stupid that he couldn't think of anything stupider to deflect attention from the thing he said yesterday. So he did what any coward would do: he fled. He ran out of the press room like Ivanka squealing in her nighty while he gives chase!

Is this the end of the daily shitshow? Stay tuned!

[After that press conference, Trump stopped appearing at corona-virus briefings, which dwindled away.)

April 26, 2020 10:10 AM

Until this week, the one thing you could safely say about all American presidents is that they managed to avoid telling their citizens to drink poison.

April 26, 2020 5:52 PM

I was looking at the sun wishing for an eclipse when it hit me: sunlight kills the virus but the sun is just TOO FAR away. Since space stuff is weightless should be very easy to tow the sun to a CLOSER position to Earth to kill all the virus faster PROBLEM SOLVED You're welcome!

April 29 2020 8:14 AM

VP Pence really wanted to wear a mask on his visit to the Mayo Clinic, but Jason his massage therapist told him it would be a sin to hide that sexy jaw line.

April 30, 2020 6:14 PM

Trump: "Our death totals, our numbers, per million people, are really very, very strong. We're very proud of the job we've done."

Me: It took Kennedy, Johnson, and Nixon 14 years in Viet Nam to sacrifice the number of Americans Trump lost in six weeks.

May 1, 2020 10:21 AM

Every time I see a story about 25 armed buffoons protesting the stay-home orders, I wish somebody would do a story on the 320 million Americans who have altered their lives and gladly stayed home to save the lives of their fellow citizens. Staying home is also a political action, even if the press fails to cover it.

May 3, 2020 7:51 PM

Trump went to the Lincoln Memorial and said he has been treated worse than Lincoln. Lincoln said he looks forward to visiting the Trump Memorial and returning the favor.

May 4, 2020 8:04 AM

Everybody's gone.

May 6, 2020 8:18 AM

The only thing worse than a wildly contagious virus that kills two thousand Americans every day would be a president* who divides the country into those who "believe" in the virus and those who don't.

May 7, 2020 6:28 PM

Trump should just relax about that valet who tested positive for Cv-19. Apparently you can't contract the virus from somebody who spits in your food every single day. It's a kind of "herd immunity" thing.

May 11, 2020 4:58 PM

I will never forget when young Barack Obama in a hut in Indonesia stirred the stewpot of his granny's famous Bat Stew and plotted his eventual revenge upon the man who would succeed him to the presidency.

May 15, 2020 9:05 AM

Here in the Kingdom of No Testing, we have no virus, no sickness, no death at all. Everything is perfectly fine here and completely normal. Except maybe a little quiet at the old folks' home. And the meatpacking plant. Come join us! Come to the Land of No Testing! Today only, 30 percent off!

May 19, 2020 9:08 PM

Joe Biden is demonstrating every day that all you have to do to prove your vast superiority to the other guy is to stay very quiet and say very little. This won't work throughout the whole campaign, but for now it appears to be a winning strategy.

Or as Napoleon put it, "Never interfere with your enemy when he is making a mistake."

May 24, 2020 9:44 AM

Trump wants to be damn sure he's on the golf course when that 100,000th American dies of Covid-19, so he has just arrived at his resort for a second day in a row. I wonder if they'll pop a little bottle of Diet Coke to celebrate #100,000 or just crack a wry joke or two? We're #1! USA!

Feb 26: American death toll: 1
May 24: American death toll: 98,740

May 25, 2020 11:18 AM

Memorial Day Limerick

He has brains, but then, so does a weevil
He's your man, if you're partial to evil
He hates those whom he fears
(Empty space between ears)
Solution? I know one. Medieval.

 Donald J. Trump ✔ @realDonaldTrump · 1h
Great reviews on our handling of Covid 19, sometimes referred to as the
China Virus. Ventilators, Testing, Medical Supply Distribution, we made a lot
of Governors look very good - And got no credit for so doing. Most
importantly, we helped a lot of great people!

💬 15.5K   ↻ 8.2K   ♡ 37.9K   ⬆

Abraham Lincoln
@SurrealALincoln

Replying to @realDonaldTrump

We are still awaiting the customer reviews of 100,000 dead Americans

4:18 PM · May 25, 2020 · Twitter Web App

May 27, 2020 8:23 AM

There's not a crime on the books in any American city that carries
an instant death penalty. But that is what white policemen dish out to
black men all the time.

How do we solve this problem? To start, every policeman in
America needs training on the concept of "you are not an executioner;
there are no crimes that require or allow you to kill a suspect unless he
is trying to kill you."

May 27, 2020 8:55 PM

Police kneel on a guy's neck and kill him? "Eh, what can you do?"

Rioters break into a Target and loot flatscreen TVs? *"Call out the National Guard!"*

May 29, 2020 8:19 AM
Carter was elected to repair the damage done by Nixon. He restored integrity to government.

Clinton was elected to repair the damage done by Reagan/Bush. He eliminated the deficit and turned the economy around.

Obama was elected to repair the damage done by Bush II. He reversed the crash of 2009 and saved the world economy.

Now Biden must be elected to repair the damage done by Trump. See a pattern?

May 31, 2020 8:54 AM
From what I saw on the news last night, it's the police who are out of control. Three months of pandemic with greatly reduced crime seems to have driven them nuts. They were shooting journalists with rubber bullets, driving their cars into crowds, shooting tear gas at people marching peacefully, and otherwise ratcheting up the violence on every side.

We have a lot of bad cops. A lot more than we thought. Abolish the bad police, or at least disarm them.

May 31, 2020 8:57 PM
The best endings seem both surprising and inevitable, like Trump hiding in a bunker, for instance.

New York Times reports the Secret Service rushed Trump to the terrorism bunker during Friday's demonstrations but have released no information on whether they did that because he started crying and begging them to.

Jun 1, 2020 7:46 AM
Trump is always wanting to do things Obama never did, and now he's really done it! Cowering in a bunker while American citizens swirled around the White House, screaming at him. Even Nixon never got to flee to a bunker! We're #1! Transition to Biden!!!

Jun 1, 2020 11:42 AM

Riots are usually started by police.

In 1965, California state troopers pulled over a man named Marquette Frye in a traffic stop that went bad. A fight broke out, police injured a pregnant woman, and Los Angeles exploded. The Watts riots lasted six days.

In 1992, four officers of the LAPD had a field day beating on a traffic stop suspect named Rodney King. Their acquittal ignited six days of riots.

Last night in Santa Monica, hundreds of cops faced off against a large crowd of completely peaceful protesters, ignoring the fact that a few blocks away, looters were running wild.

Police start riots.

Jun 1, 2020 6:04 PM

Trump just had peaceful protesters gassed in front of the White House so that he could go to St. John's church for a photo opportunity.

In the Rose Garden, as the flash-bangs and tear gas canisters exploded in the background, he announced he will use the "Insurrection Act" of 1807 to send American troops into American streets to fight American people.

William Barr came out to check the troops before the battle began.

Jun 5, 2020 3:23 PM

When a white man says "I can't breathe," he means it is inconvenient to wear a mask to prevent the spread of the virus.

When a black man says "I can't breathe," he means the white man is kneeling on his neck.

Jun 8, 2020 8:14 AM

I wish my liberal friends were one-tenth as concerned about the crimes being committed by the police as they are about the slogan "defund the police."

Jun 9, 2020 12:14 PM

Today I'm so excited because Mr. Soros is flying myself (and others in my cadre) to the secret location of his Antifa Training Compound. I will be learning advanced radical techniques such as falling faster than I have been pushed, bleeding spontaneously from the ears, and scanning police communication devices with my hands to render them useless. I am being well paid, of course - they hand us all a black Visa card when we board the big Airbus. Wish me luck, friends - I have a lot to learn to become a real Antifa! Fight the power!

Jun 11, 2020 11:14 AM

If you want to attend the Trump rally in Tulsa, you have to click on this disclaimer to say you won't sue if you get Covid-19 and die. The people will click, and they will eagerly flock to the rally even at the risk of their lives . . . and isn't that the dictionary definition of a cult?

By clicking register below, you are acknowledging that an inherent risk of exposure to COVID-19 exists in any public place where people are present. By attending the Rally, you and any guests voluntarily assume all risks related to exposure to COVID-19 and agree not to hold Donald J. Trump for President, Inc.; BOK Center; ASM Global; or any of their affiliates, directors, officers, employees, agents, contractors, or volunteers liable for any illness or injury.

Jun 12, 2020 8:23 PM

From my Twitter friend Aiden Wolfe: "Say what ya want about the Obamas, but Michelle never had to take a year long tax payer funded sabbatical to re-negotiate a prenup because the sight of her husband's naked flesh caused her to sob so hard that a fortune in facial stitches began popping and leaking toxic chemicals."

Jun 13, 2020 9:45 AM

Now it can be told: I took a Coronavirus Road Trip in May, and here's the essay I wrote about it for the Wall Street Journal.

A Road Trip Across the Southwest in the Time of Coronavirus

On a Tuesday in mid-May, pandemic rules in New Orleans were relaxed enough to permit dentists to resume practice, so I went in for my checkup.

When the masked-and-gowned technician touched my arm I realized she was the first human being to touch me in eight weeks.

For some reason, this gave me a terrible urge to get out of town.

I needed a road trip. Couldn't talk anyone into riding shotgun, but who cares? Alone on the road is no lonelier than alone at home, and the scenery is better. Coming from a city that was an early hotspot, I'd been totally isolating myself, so I was pretty sure I wasn't a spreader. The Mayor lifted her stay-home order just in time to keep me from going pure crazy.

I flew to San Francisco on an airplane full of people with masks trying not to breathe. We staggered out of the plane wondering what happened to the idea they would be leaving the middle seats empty. But masks were required and everybody wore one. Except the guy who stepped onto the rental-car bus just as the doors closed behind him. He sneezed without covering his mouth. I sat in my mask watching his droplets fill the bus. I held my breath for seven minutes, a world record. I squirted hand sanitizer onto every exposed part of my body.

I rented a car and started driving. I wanted to go to the parts of the country where nobody is. First, you have to get through California. The south shore of Lake Tahoe on a sunny Saturday was crowded with people who, like me, just had to get out of the house, even if only in the car.

I stopped at a Safeway to buy survival snacks in case I was stranded in the Nevada desert. Everybody in the store was wearing a mask. California has many kinds of jerky.

I passed out of California to the busy areas around Carson City, the town of Fallon where the Top Gun pilots fly up and down long desert valleys. I felt the pandemic lifting up as the civilization thinned out. Where there are no people there is no infection. It's an odd fact of pandemic life that you find yourself longing for human contact while wishing for a place where there's nobody within miles of you.

Shortly past Fallon, a sign says "Next Gas 80 Miles" and brother they ain't kidding. Not only no gas but no tree no blade of grass no shack no fence no nothing nothing nothing. Just open land and space and air. I stopped the car in the middle of the road. You can see 10 miles in each direction and I saw that I was alone. The silent emptiness was glorious. I turned off the car and stood there taking in deep breaths of unpopulated air.

I detoured half a mile to see the ancient petroglyphs, and 10 miles to see the earthquake faults. I chewed jerky and listened to Rachmaninoff and Bessie Smith. I did not wear a mask in the car. I spewed my own droplets, but only upon myself.

For the next three days I suffered every symptom of COVID-19 in my head. Thanks, maskless sneezer on the bus! Scratchy throat. Pounding headache. Is that shortness of breath? (Yes, it is – look at the sign – I'm at an altitude of 9,000 feet.) Is that twinge in my side a result of too much jerky, or the first sign of the virus that will take me down in some godforsaken saloon of a hospital where no one will care when I die?

The first night in Ely, Nevada, capital of the middle of nowhere, the motel desk lady wore her mask as she told me where to find takeout Mexican food, in the back of the casino. The dowdy little casino was silent but the takeout business was thriving.

The next day was Utah. Utah is blessed with more scenery than anywhere else. Almost every part of Utah looks like a national park. There were no people anywhere until I got near Zion National Park, near Springdale, in southwestern Utah. Unbeknownst to me, Zion was one of the first national parks to reopen. Suddenly it was a busy summer weekend, carloads of people stopped at every turnout, snapping pics.

I rolled on through. I stopped once in awhile for gas or a stretch. Utah just keeps giving up the scenery. The trip took on a random character. I drove out of my way to see Mountain Meadows, where a bunch of Mormon settlers disguised themselves as Native Americans for the purpose of attacking and slaughtering an entire wagon train full of men, women, and children, for no particular reason.

I spent that night in a Holiday Inn in Grand Junction, Colo. On this trip, I avoided any place with the slightest charm, and stuck to the chain motels following CDC protocols for sanitation. Every place I stayed was wildly over sanitized, with nice careful employees, and the rooms almost completely empty. Also, I brought my own pillow. I wish you could open motel windows for fresh air, but I felt safe and didn't get sick (knock wood).

I stuck to two-lanes. Got off the interstate in California and stayed off until Texas. In the small towns along U.S. 50, only the gas stations were open, and a little supermarket now and then.

The next day, snow-capped mountains again: Colorado. I had planned my route to include the excitement of driving the Million-Dollar Highway. I like driving mountain roads. I have driven terrifying roads in Costa Rica, Jamaica, Peru, and Italy. Let me tell you, the Million-Dollar Highway is a winner. Going south, you're on the outside of the curves. I had to stop in the middle of the road just to calm myself and breathe. I would not let myself look over the several-thousand-foot drop off with no guardrails. Boom boom boom well at least my heart is still working, good show! No COVID in this heart, no siree!

I clutched the wheel so tightly that part of my knuckles are still in Colorado. After a couple of hours of pulse pounding, the miles to Durango and on to Santa Fe were relaxing.

For these days I just drove and drove. I took the long way around. I made unnecessary detours to avoid larger towns. I stopped once to look at a sparkly thing in the road. It turned out not to be gold.

I kept thinking I would find somewhere to eat, but the few places that were open looked too crowded. I knew when I set out I wouldn't be making this trip for the fine dining. I did have a perfectly delicious sausage and biscuit from McDonald's because there was nothing else within 30 miles. I ate convenience-store snacks. Mostly jerky, the pioneer treat.

At night, I tried to find a nice dinner, but the places that were supposed to be open were closed. Three nights in a row I wound up with the same indistinguishable Mexican food in an aluminum take-out plate, eaten in the motel room with my cheerful dining companion, Anderson Cooper.

Everybody in California wore masks. In Nevada, a few people did. In Utah, nobody. In Colorado, everybody. In New Mexico, about half. In Texas, nobody nowhere. Other than that, I can report that things were the same all over: quiet.

From Santa Fe, the rest of New Mexico rolls out attractively, mesa and range, looking like its postcards, right up to the very state line – then suddenly it becomes Texas, and all interest ceases. The land flattens out and loses geological appeal. From the Texas border to New Orleans is a 14-hour marathon interstate run with no place to stop.

Finally it's Louisiana at last and it's green, with big trees, a swamp, more swamp. New Orleans. Good to be home. I go into my house, take off my mask. I flip on the TV. The pandemic's still going, and people are mad at each other. But I don't feel so trapped any more. America is a big place. Big enough for all of us, even on days when it sure doesn't feel like that.

Jun 19, 2020 7:56 AM

In America today if you are president* in the middle of a pandemic and you get restless because it's been months since your followers showered you with adulation, you can get 20,000 people to risk their own lives to attend a superspreader event, while also risking the lives of thousands more people, in a hopeless attempt to fill the bottomless hole of your need...and *no one will be able to stop you.*

Jun 21, 2020 10:12 AM

He was so sure "the Legend of the Ramp" would go over big. He did it on the plane going out, and everybody howled. He thought it would be the big comic centerpiece of the show. Also he practiced SO HARD to drink the water. All week long he practiced that. And he drank the water. Did not spill a drop! And he did it with one hand - Which nobody thought he could do! But then he knew his hand was about to start trembling so he flung the water and glass away from him. And then he remembered a few more things he needed to tell about the Ramp.

Jun 24, 2020 8:38 PM

A hymn

They want to throw God's wonderful breathing system out the door
They want to make us forget what God made mouths and noses for

It's enough to make God scratch his holy head and say
Keep that mask right off your face, you won't get sick today!

Jun 25, 2020 4:15 PM
New Orleans is a blue dot in red Louisiana. We are a tourist town – that's our only industry except for oil, which is also in a depression. We were hit hard early on in this pandemic. We shut down completely for months. The city of New Orleans has done a very good job of flattening the curve, but Louisiana's numbers are rising again because many Republicans live there, and won't wear their masks or change their diapers. So Louisiana is stuck in Phase 2 for now.

Jun 25, 2020 9:05 PM
Biden today, on Trump: "He's like a child who can't believe this has happened to him. All his whining and self- pity. Well, this pandemic didn't happen to him, it happened to all of us. And his job isn't to whine about it. His job is to do something about it."

Jun 27, 2020 11:45 AM
Putin paid the Taliban to murder American soldiers. Trump found out months ago. His response was to invite Putin to join the G7.

Jun 28, 2020 8:56 AM
A day when the man posing as president* retweets a video of his supporters yelling "White power! White power!" and no one at the White House takes it down, and you think about how many years the media has spent toying with the question of whether it's okay to call him a racist.

Jun 30, 2020 9:04 PM
Joe Biden could shoot me in the middle of Fifth Avenue and I would apologize to him for using up one of his bullets, and then I would crawl on my hands and knees to the polling place to vote for him on Nov. 3.

Jun 30, 2020 9:33 PM

Trump wasn't briefed about Russia putting out hits on our soldiers.
He was briefed but he didn't hear it.
He heard it but he didn't understand it.
He understood it but he forgot about it.
He forgot about it and no one reminded him.
No one reminded him because they didn't want to tell him.
They didn't want to tell him because he doesn't listen.
Trump wasn't briefed about Russia putting out hits on our soldiers.
See how it works?
[NARRATOR: He was briefed.]

Jul 3, 2020 7:43 AM

Friend and I talking last night about the Biden "basement" strategy. We observed that Biden's polls have been rising slightly during this period but that "Trump's" polls are cratering.

It's not just that Trump is killing himself with his demented pandemic antics, although he is. I think one of the smart unspoken messages Biden is giving us is "elect me and you will have your tv back, you won't have to watch breaking news every day, I won't be all over the internet and dominating the battlespace everywhere you turn."

In other words, his implicit promise is to shut up, do his job, and give us back our normal lives.

He'll have to step out more as the campaign goes on. But this factor, and being the guy NOT hosting super-spreader campaign events, are definite pluses for right now.

Jul 4, 2020 3:31 PM

If only we hadn't counted them, those 130,000 Americans would still be alive.

Donald J. Trump ✓
@realDonaldTrump

Cases, Cases, Cases! If we didn't test so much and so successfully, we would have very few cases. If you test 40,000,000 people, you are going to have many cases that, without the testing (like other countries), would not show up every night on the Fake Evening News.....

1:49 PM · Jul 4, 2020   ⓘ

♡ 143.1K   ♡ 89K people are Tweeting about this

Jul 4, 2020 8:31 PM

Happy Fourth of July! Trump made us so Great that Americans are currently barred from traveling to almost every country in the world. We've never been THAT Great before!

Next time some Trumper tells me to move to some other country if I hate America so much, I'm going to have to point out that no country on earth will admit Americans right now. So they're stuck with me.

Jul 4, 2020 9:08 PM

Kanye West says he's running for president. Untreated bipolar disorder, meet malignant narcissism + frontotemporal dementia! This is just 2020 showing off like, You thought I was all fucked up yesterday and it couldn't get any worse? Check this out! Kanye for President AND murder hornets!

Jul 5, 2020 11:40 AM

The ones who won't wear a mask are all about their freedom, with the result that the rest of us will remain prisoners in our own homes.

They have done this because Trump has abandoned the fight against Covid and is messaging "we must learn to live with it." In other words, the new strategy is the strategy Trump used back when he called the virus a hoax: "Most of you won't die."

Jul 8, 2020 7:46 AM

Great statements in White House history:

Kayleigh McInanity: "I have yet to see the (Bolton) book, but it is a book of falsehoods."

FDR: "Fear is a hoax"

JFK: "We already went to the moon - it was awesome"

Lincoln: "Stick around for act III of 'Our American Cousin' – hilarious!"

Jul 8, 2020 3:11 PM

If I was Joe Biden, which I'm not, I would call up Anthony Fauci right now and say "quit your job, stop trying to talk sense to the lunatic, come aboard as my pandemic advisor and I'll let you give daily briefings on your own, saying whatever you want to say. And when I'm elected, you stay in the White House to direct pandemic response, as long as it takes."

New surge of virus cases in Tulsa just 14 days after Trump had his rally there. He's planning lots more rallies.

Jul 8, 2020 4:53 PM

Hey I know! Instead of reopening the schools, Trump can just pay somebody to take everybody's tests for them.

Jul 9, 2020 5:44 PM

Americans natter on about how much they love home and family, but a lot of them would literally rather die than stay home with those families being bored a few more weeks. If these people were the Donner Party, they'd have eaten each other the first time it snowed.

Jul 12, 2020 6:40 PM

If Hillary Clinton were president today, there would be 137,000 more Americans alive now, and they would all be bitching about President Hillary Clinton.

Jul 13, 2020 8:45 AM

The Washington Redskins are looking for a new name. Suggestions:

Washington Genocidals
Washington Manifest Destinies
Washington Wounded Knees
Washington Bighorns (take that, Custer!)
Washington Former Slaveholders
Washington Whatabouts

Jul 13, 2020 7:25 PM

The latest casualty of the Trump Virus is K-Paul's Louisiana Kitchen on Chartres Street, which announced its closing today after a spectacular run since 1979.

When I first met Paul in 1981, the restaurant was a small homely space in a long narrow former hardware store. Paul was a big man from Opelousas, down in Cajunland. He laughed at us for thinking we could learn about Cajun food in New Orleans. "Rent the biggest car they got, and I'll take you where to eat," he said.

For the next three days the photographer and I drove him around in a Lincoln Town Car, stopping every hour or two to eat. We ate in his aged aunt's kitchen, catfish shacks, roadside boudin stands, the backs of grocery stores and fancy restaurants where Paul was treated as a god. I gained ten pounds in three days. Paul said there was a fat man inside me and he would help get him out. (It worked!)

When our story about Paul was published in Southern Living, one of the readers was Nancy Reagan, who called up Paul and invited him to cater a Presidential summit at Williamsburg, Virginia. Paul always credited that job with putting him on the map nationally. So he was grateful to me. Every time I ever ate in his restaurant for the next 34 years, as long as he was alive, I never had to wait in line and I never got a check.

Paul died in 2015 and the restaurant carried on, but he was always the soul of the place. Goodbye, K-Paul's! I will miss you.

Jul 14, 2020 10:09 AM

Sometimes it's important to note the little milestones. Like, it's kind of sad to think that we will never ever get to see Trump try to walk down a ramp in public again.

Ivanka Trump ✔ @IvankaTrump · 22m
If it's Goya, it has to be good.
Si es Goya, tiene que ser bueno.

Jul 15, 2020 8:45 AM

I am become Death, the destroya
Of all I behold, even Goya
My Dad loves these beans
Like the back of my jeans
And I posed for this just to annoya

Jul 15, 2020 1:58 PM

Fox News reports that Kanye West has ended his campaign for the presidency. Man, that was quicker than Trump on Stormy! All I can say is, we hardly knew Ye.

In related news: I have ended my bid to become the King of the Moon.

Jul 17, 2020 4:41 PM

Just thought I'd mention that Trump has a secret police force in camouflage roaming around Portland arresting people randomly while refusing to identify themselves OK let's go back to laughing about the Goya photo.

Jul 18, 2020 7:22 AM

The greatest living Alabamian is dead. John Lewis was too good to survive this particular world.

Long live John Lewis! Long may he march for justice. He's walking with Rosa Parks and C.T. Vivian and Martin and Ralph and Fannie Lou and all the heroes who went before him.

Jul 23, 2020 5:01 PM

Bill Barr is the Sean Spicer of Heinrich Himmlers.

Jul 23, 2020 7:02 PM

Too dangerous for Republicans to convene in Jacksonville, but get those schools open RIGHT NOW! Only a "tiny tiny amount" of children will die! Chances are it won't be your kid!   Suck it up, snowflake parents!

Jul 24, 2020 10:44 AM
My mother used to brag about how she aced the cognitive test too, as Trump just did, but after they moved her to the dementia ward she pretty much forgot about it.

Jul 28, 2020 10:06 AM
Republicans say it's just as easy for people to live on $200 a week as on $600. If you run short of money you can always rent out your vacation home, or sell some of your old Prada shoes on Ebay.

Jul 28, 2020 3:27 PM
The problem with creating a media system that lies to you for 30 years is that when the deadly pandemic starts and you really need people to believe and act on the truth, they can't do it. They've forgotten how to respond to the truth. All they know is how to twist it into a conspiracy theory.

Jul 28, 2020 4:51 PM
Trump on Dr. Fauci: "He's got this high approval rating...Why don't I have a high approval rating?...Nobody likes me. It could only be my personality. I don't know."

Jul 29, 2020 8:13 AM
Somebody on Facebook got mad last night and told me Joe Biden is a "bafune," and I just didn't have a good answer.

Jul 30, 2020 7:13 AM
He has no power to delay the election.   Republicans? I can't hear you.

Donald J. Trump ✔
@realDonaldTrump

With Universal Mail-In Voting (not Absentee Voting, which is good), 2020 will be the most INACCURATE & FRAUDULENT Election in history. It will be a great embarrassment to the USA. Delay the Election until people can properly, securely and safely vote???

7:46 AM · Jul 30, 2020   ⓘ

Jul 30, 2020 11:43 AM

It was announced today that Trump's African-American supporter Herman Cain died of Covid, about a month after appearing at Trump's Tulsa rally without a mask. Darwin is a strict teacher and gives no extra points for sucking up to the boss.

Aug 6, 2020 1:43 PM

Trump on Covid: "This thing's going away. It will go away like things go away"

THINGS THAT GO AWAY:
1. Your daughter, when you're chasing her in your boxers
2. Your campaign managers, when they are sent to prison
3. Your hair, inexorably
4. Synonyms for "things that go away"
5. Your faculties

Aug 8, 2020 8:01 PM

Yes, Trump finally got his wall. The rest of the world built it. It surrounds the USA on all sides.

This wall doesn't keep others out, it keeps us in. Walls us up in our infected, infectious, disease-ridden nation. The Trump Wall is complete. His greatest achievement. We are Covid America.

Every 80 seconds another American dies of the virus. "Fifteen cases, soon going to zero" is now, officially: five million cases. 165,088 deaths. More Americans have died of Covid-19 than all the people who died in Hiroshima and Nagasaki.

Aug 9, 2020 2:51 PM

I'm sure it's a joke that Trump wants to put himself on Mt. Rushmore, but just in case, I am taking a "Great Courses" in "How to Obtain and Operate a Surface-to-Surface Missile."

Aug 11, 2020 8:22 AM

FutureSpeech™

The Second Gettysburg Address

Eighty seven years ago
People mistreated me very strongly.
A bunch of old men got together.
But who cares what they did?
I alone can fix it.
If I didn't ban the China Virus, it would be
Everywhere now.
We would have the worst pandemic in the world instead of
The best, which is what we have.
Cases Not Deaths. You can't do that.
Lucky for you I am very.
Stable. Genius. Person. Man. Woman. Camera. TV.
Four more me!
Yo! Semite!
World War II!
Make America Bad Again To Be Great Again Next Year

Aug 11, 2020 9:41 AM

Just so you won't be surprised, Vice-Presidential nominee Kamala Harris is Obama's sister from Kenya, she killed Vince Foster, and taught Hillary how to shoot the guns that were used at Benghazi.

Aug 18, 2020 7:41 PM

Yeah yeah Jill Biden you're a school teacher, but did you ever pose naked while pretending to eat a bowl of diamonds?

Aug 28 8:47 PM

"The only thing we have to fear is fear itself." - FDR

"You know what I say? Protestors, your ass. I don't talk about my ass."
                                                    - Trump tonight in New Hampshire

Aug 19, 2020 8:14 AM

I'm old enough to remember when you could post a picture of the First Lady with no fear of getting banned from Twitter.

Aug 20, 2020 10:38 AM

"Steve Bannon Arrested!" has a jaunty rollicking beat, like "Surrey With the Fringe on Top."

Aug 20, 2020 9:58 PM

Brayden Harrington is the kid with the stutter, my new hero. His speech at the Democratic National Convention was great. And Joe Biden is right now in the middle of giving the best speech of his whole goddamn life.

He's a real guy. A great guy. With flaws. But good. He's our next President.

Aug 21, 2020 3:36 PM

They're gonna have a very busy week!

EMBARGOED Not For Release EYES ONLY
Tentative Schedule GOP Convention Charlotte NC 2020

MONDAY
8 - Invocation and Blessing - Jerry Falwell, Jr. - "Unzipped By My Lord"
  8:15 - video presentation "Kids In Cages United Choir" sings "Guantanamera"
8:30 pm - 8:31 pm. Liz Cheney - "Ladies and Gentlemen, If I May, Let Me Just"
8:31-9 pm Sen Lindsey Graham - "Rough Tough Unshaven Gardeners Are the Future of Democracy"
9-9:15 pm Silk performs "Why I Hate Diamond"
9:15-9:30 pm Diamond performs "Silk Is Fake News"
9:30-10 pm Keynote: Sen. Marco Rubio - "I Have Never Met Matt Gaetz's Son Nestor"

TUESDAY
8-8:15 - Tim Allen - "Right Wing Humor: The Chicken Had to Build That Road Before He Could Cross It"
8:30-9 pm Kid Rock - "My Greatest Hit Played Several Times with a Choir of Tiny Live Mexicans"
9-9:15 Sec of State Mike Pompeo - "When To Expect the Nuclear Holocaust [Armageddon]"
9:15-9:30 Eastwood's chair, interviewed by Tucker Carlson "The Chair Talks Back"
9:30-9:31 Victoria Jackson looks back on her career
9:31-10 pm, Keynote Sen. Susan Collins - "Sidestroking Through the Deep End of My Concern"

WEDNESDAY
8-8:15 Eric Trump leads a workshop in construction paper folding, coloring for pleasure
8:15-8:29 Sarah Huckabee Sanders - "That's Why God Gave Me Eye to See"

8:29-8:30 Tiffany Trump introduces Ivanka Trump
8:30-8:45 Ivanka Trump - "The Smell of Daddy"
8:45-9:15 Kayleigh McEnany - "I Will Never Lie To You From Now On, Starting Now"
9:15-9:16 Mike Pence introduces FLOTUS
9:16-11:45 pm - Rose Garden - Melania Trump performs a ballet while phonetically reading speeches by Eleanor Roosevelt

THURSDAY
8-8:15 Donald Trump Jr. "Why I Get to Go on Thursday Night Instead of Wednesday - I'm His Favorite Is Why!"
8:15-8:30 Barron Trump - "I Have Learned to Stutter Too"
8:30-8:45 - remote - Bob Dole dragged from his bed by a pack of young goons and beaten to death, musical medley by "Lady Antebellum"
8:45-9 pm Stephen Miller - "Stop Calling Me Woolly Willy or Meet Your Doom, America"
9-9:05 Re-enactment of White House funeral of dead Trump brother [name? TK]
9:05-9:10 Vladimir Putin introduces Donald J Trump
9:10-10 pm Donald J. Trump [extemporaneous} "Yo Semite, Fatilitics, and Thighland, or: Hey Lady, Let Me Grab You By the Covfefe"

Aug 22, 2020 8:33 AM
   If we have two hurricanes wandering around the Gulf, and one of them has to be named "Marco," for God's sake the other one must be called "Polo."

Aug 22, 2020 4:58 PM
   "Everyone is talking me how ugly is my new Rose Garden. They is talking Jackie O made better Rose Garden. Only Jackie O was bornt before high spike heel. She know nothing! If she had high spike heel she wood Put sidewalk in Rose Garden! Also she is too old now and dead. I really don't care about her, why do u?
   "Was before only trees old trees and too many color. All so colors! I like red Christmas tree all red. Or all black tree. Not some green and

some red and then other things. Peoples in this country has Too many color! Like Chinese. Look at my dress. Is black. Or is blue. Is not BLACK AND BLUE.

"Landscape Butler says Ma'am what is your choice here? What like you? I show contact sheets from shoot in Gstaad after Brazilian wax. I tell him 'Butler, This is it I want! More naked garden, see? So you can see the bones. Now my Rose Garden is clean and has good shave."

Aug 24, 2020 11:47 AM

Not content with taking the top speaking slot for all four nights of his "convention," Trump is now on stage speaking to the Republicans about what a great job he did on the pandemic.

Wonder if he'll do his droning prompter Thighland act every night, or if he'll do Drunk Grandpa Ramble.

Not sure why they don't just let him be on TV for every damn slot of the whole four days. Since he is the party and they are he. The GOP just did away with 250 years of party tradition and jettisoned their entire party platform in favor of one that consists of "We Love Our Emperor and His Magnificent Robes."

Aug 24, 2020 9:02 PM

ONCE I GOT STUCK ON AN AIRPLANE NEXT TO KIMBERLY GUILFOYLE WHEN SHE WAS STILL MARRIED TO GAVIN NEWSOM AND I SWEAR THIS IS EXACTLY HOW LOUD SHE TALKED ON HER CELLPHONE

...and after watching Don Jr.'s convention speech, I think they should give equal time to Pepsi.

Aug 25, 2020 1:06 PM

Last night Nikki Haley said America is not a racist nation. But if that's true, why doesn't she use her real name, Nimrata?

Aug 26 8:50 PM

The Republicans say I won't be safe in Joe Biden's America but I've been locked in my house for six months, so...

"You must elect Trump to save the nation from the chaos and violence of the current administration" is the entire Republican platform.

Aug 27, 2020 9:14 PM

In case you didn't see it, tonight your house, the White House, the People's House, was dolled up in campaign frittery and Trump-Pence signs, and used as a Republican campaign setting. Our house, dolled up in a tawdry gown like a whore, the place spangled up with signs like a used-car lot.

Aug 28, 2020 2:17 PM

Don Junior high, ratings low, Melania's wild look of Ivanka-hate, droning Donald, bellowing Guilfoyle, superspreader illegal lawn party rally, White House gussied up as a floozy, wild-eyed white men, Ben Carson, free pardons, live naturalizations, Fish Boy, Snake Girl - did I miss anything? Farewell, Republican National Convention 2020!

Aug 31, 2020 8:58 AM

Anybody seen a "leftist demonstrator" arrested for using a weapon at a demonstration? If not, why not? Who is actually causing the violence? Why do the New York Times, Washington Post, and cable news networks continue to frame the violence as "police vs. protesters" when the only ones showing up with guns are Trump supporters?

"Antifa" must be the only resistance movement in history with no leaders, no spokesmen, no members getting arrested, no publicly stated cause, and an aversion to publicity?

This false flag operation is familiar to students of 1929-1933. Hint: they wore brown shirts instead of red hats.

Sep 1, 2020 11:33 AM

We've now reached the part of this story where every daily newscast will contain some discussion of the crazy stuff that the president* said today, and whether it is an indication that he himself is crazy, senile, addled, drugged, or some combination of all these.

In today's edition, he says there are plane loads of anarchists in dark uniforms flying into Republican cities to start wars.

Sep 2, 2020 8:33 AM
[Trump says Portland protesters came armed with "cans of soup" as weapons.]

Armed with one last desperate bag of Chicken Noodle, Bean with Bacon, and Creams of both Mushroom and Celery, dear Mother, we have left the safety of our Bowling Green encampment and are advancing on the revolutionary airports of Portland!

Sep 2, 2020 1:38 PM
Hey Soros Squad: The Righties have caught on to our Soup Tactic which may make it hard for some of you to board ThugAir flights to destroy GOP cities.

Here are some ways to get our canned soup weapons past the TSA:

1. Put them in a baby carriage with a picture of a baby
2. Put them in your sweat pants and tell the TSA officer you are "genetically lumpy"
3. Tell the TSA officer they are cans of beans, not soup
4. Distract the TSA officer with a sexually inviting pose, then strike him or her with a can of Chicken Noodle (a classic soup)
5. Tape the cans to your inner thighs and waddle right through the checkpoint
6. Print and apply "Trump Soup" labels to the cans - you'll get express lane valet service!

If you are having trouble accessing your cash through your Soros ProtestACard, please contact your control officer at any DeepState location.

Sep 2, 2020 6:34 PM

Finally I understand. Ivanka is "the other First Lady," just as pork is "the other white meat."

Sep 3, 2020 3:40 PM

Secret Bulletin: Eyes Only

From: Soros/Anarchy HQ
Attention all,
The first meeting of the Anarchist Rules Committee will take place tonight.
Place: Wherever you feel like. You're an anarchist.
Time: Totally up to you.

Sep 3, 2020 6:54 PM

Today he told a crowd at a Pennsylvania hangar that he likes the hangar events because "I don't have to travel" and "I just make a speech, then I get the hell out of here." The crowd cheered.
Also, the soldiers killed in wars are "suckers" and "losers" and he didn't want amputee soldiers in his parade because "nobody wants to see that."

Sep 4, 2020 7:14 PM

Trump has decided that instead of shutting down "Stars and Stripes" he'll just change its name to "Suckers and Losers."

Sep 5, 2020 9:12 PM

Today a Trump boat parade in Texas ended with at least four vessels sunk and many Trump supporters in the lake. Luckily, no one drowned. With no apology whatever to Gordon Lightfoot.

THE WRECK OF THE 'SS FULL MAGA'

The legend lives on from Bowling Green on down
Of the big lake they called Sinky Trumpy
Lake Travis, it's said, never gives up her dead
When the lakes of September turn bumpy

With a load of full bores, twenty six thousand tons more
Than the 'SS Full MAGA' weighed empty
That good ship and true painted red white and blue
When the waves of November came early

The ship was the pride of the north Dallas burbs
Sailing back from a rally in Irving
As motorboats go, it was bigger than most
With a captain and crew - more than twenty

Their MAGA hats on, but of masks, they had none
When they left fully loaded for Austin
And later that night when the ship's bell rang
Could it be the blue wave they'd been lost in?

With covfefe strong, all the boats sailed along
Flying Trump flags from every railing
The waves rose up high but they zoomed right on by
All the libtards alongshore, a-wailing

And every man knew, as the captain did too,
Twas the witch of November come stealing!
Kamala's her name and they see her dark flame
Lighting up the skies o'er Sinky Trumpy

The boats were too close - two or three feet at most
And the big waves began now a buildin-
The little boats sank, people fell in and drank

The dark waters of gloomy Lake Travis

When suppertime came the old man came on deck sayin
Magas, it's too rough to feed ya
But at 7 pm when the hatchway caved in, he said
Magas, it's been good to know ya!

The captain, he cried out to call 9-1-1
But his phone could not get a signal
He sent off a text and he tried WhatsApp next
But the good ship and crew were in peril

And later that night when his lights went outta sight
Came the wreck of the SS Full MAGA
Does anyone know where a Trumper can go
To find someone to hear his sad saga?

The searchers all say they'd have made it that day
If they hadn't drunk so much Sam Adams
Of twenty white men, none that knew how to swim
We searched for 'em deep in the fathoms

They might have split up or they might have got swamped
It might have been sharks that have got 'em
Now all that remains is the faces and the names
And the Trump flags stretched out on the bottom

The legend lives on from Bowling Green on down
Of the big lake they called Sinky Trumpy
Lake Travis, they said, never gives up her dead
When the waves of November come early!

Sep 9, 2020 9:38 AM
     Trump and Bill Barr are moving to let your Justice Department
take over the defense of Trump in a rape case that happened in the

1990s. The argument is that Trump defamed his rape victim while he was president*, so the DOJ can defend him for that. Keep in mind, they argue that Trump can commit any crime while president* and cannot be indicted for it.

Today they seek to claim that we all must pay to defend him for any crimes he committed at any time in his life! as long as he talked about it while he was president*....

I recognize this is a Legal Maneuver that is likely to fail, but I just wanted to pause and remark on the utter degradation of this man. Just because he hits a new low every day doesn't mean we should not discuss every single new low. Outlast and outlive this son of a bitch.

Sep 9, 2020 8:38 PM

Bob Woodward reveals: Trump knew many thousands of Americans would die because he was downplaying the virus, but he gambled. And we lost.

He played it down, all right: because he and Jared thought it was killing a lot more in blue states than in red states, and they were just fine with that.

Sep 28, 2020 4:05 PM

We should give Brad Parscale the same consideration we would give any shirtless raging heavily-armed money-laundering fascist Trump campaign manager who beats his wife and has friends on the police force to make sure he doesn't get killed while being arrested.

Sep 29, 2020 9:43 PM

Who Am I? .... I have $400 million in debt but I won't tell you who I owe. I am above the law because my attorney general is a stooge. I've killed 200,000 of my constituents and I'm running for a second term. I pay my daughter $700k a year and deduct it as a business expense.

Sep 29, 2020 10:44 PM

Biden won the shitshow debate by being the only man on that stage who wasn't intimidated by Donald Trump.

Everybody on the teevee is acting as if we should call off the remaining debates because Trump can't behave himself and follow the rules. Giving in to bullies makes them bolder. He lost the debate, badly. Let's give him two more debates just like it.

It is important that the American people be forced to face evidence of the man occupying the most powerful office in the world. It is important that they see what they did by installing him.

Joe Biden told Trump to his face that he is the worst president* in American history. And then he asked him to shut up. So I sent Joe fifty bucks.

Oct 2, 2020 1 PM
[Trump is diagnosed with Covid-19]

TRUMP: Hack hack hack *splat*
MELANIA: (small ladylike cough)
TRUMP: Hack hack hack *splat*
MELANIA: Oh for God sake stop coughing you are worse than fucking Christmas
TRUMP: Hack hack hack *splat*
MELANIA: How are you infect me, you fucking loser
TRUMP: Hack hack hack *splat* shut up
MELANIA: Sickness-health clause, see prenup addendum B subparagraph L, bonus payment due by midnight tonight

Oct 3, 2020 8:19 AM
For those of us who've hunkered at home and behind masks for 7 months, the spectacle of all these White House people falling ill after mocking us for our "fear" and our masks provokes wildly mixed feelings of sympathy and satisfaction. I hope they all make a full recovery ... *after* they've learned a lesson.

Oct 3, 2020 8:29 AM

TRUMP: Hello? Hello? Hack hack hack *splat*.

MELANIA: Vat you vant?

TRUMP: Hey, is this my number one First Lady?

MELANIA: You calling me? Vot the hell you vant?

TRUMP: They say I'm pretty sick. They say I might die.

MELANIA: OK

TRUMP: Somebody was saying - not me, but a lot of people are saying maybe it would be better if you came over to the hospital. You know, the whole wife thing.

MELANIA: Off with your fuck, my nose is walking like a dog! You this did me! Your fault one dozen percent! My eyes swoll so much, I see barely! I look so bad! Like your first or second wife! Or third!

TRUMP: Fine. Fine. Don't come. I'll just die.

MELANIA: Don't calling this number again.

Oct 3, 2020 10:12 AM

Any parent (Amy Covid Barrett) who doesn't have the sense not to bring her seven children maskless to a crowded photo-op event during a pandemic does not have the judgment to sit on the Supreme Court.

Oct 4, 2020 8:41 AM

TRUMP: TV is saying I might be dead or I might be fine

MELANIA: I really don't care, do U?

TRUMP: This place is a dump

MELANIA: I be to go now. Sale at Zappo.

TRUMP: They don't even have hamberders, or so they claim

MELANIA: Don't call this number again

TRUMP: Hack hack *splat*

Oct 4, 2020 4:40 PM

Go in your house, lock the doors and windows. That crazy MF has busted out of Walter Reed and is driving around spreading his infection in a great cloud of superspreader droplets. Or else he was just faking all along....

I'm not sure I'd want to enrage and endanger the very Secret Service agents surrounding me at all times and charged with protecting my life. Especially with all those handy pillows lying around.

Oct 5, 2020 8:21 AM

TRUMP: Did you see my drive-by?
MELANIA: Who this is?
TRUMP: All the cable channels carried it live. The ratings will be HUGE. Hack hack hack *splat*
MELANIA: How got you this number?
TRUMP: You can buy all the burner phones in the world, it won't help - the White House switchboard is the best in the world.
MELANIA: What wanting you? I'm busy
TRUMP: My hands looked HUGE in the Chevy Suburban. Bigger than they look in the limo. I'm gonna use the Chevy from now on. Hack hack hack *splat*
MELANIA: You stay hospital. Not be coming here. You sick motha.
TRUMP: Read the prenup. You gotta meet the chopper on the South Lawn or NO BONUS.
MELANIA: I'm sick too, you hole of ass!
TRUMP: Whatever, just get out to that chopper.

Oct 5, 2020 11:59 AM

Super-covid-mask-denying-trump-infecta-tosis
Even though the sound of it is something quite atrocious
If you breathe his droplets in, you'll get the diagnosis
Super-covid-mask-denying-trump-infecta-tosis!

Oct 6, 2020 8:03 PM
Stephen Miller has Covid. Hi's doctor reports that he is resting comfortably, hanging by his feet from the ceiling.

Oct 7, 2020 6:08 PM

Trump says catching Covid-19 was a "blessing from God" because he's such a genius that he prescribed himself "Regeneron" (the name of the manufacturer, not the drug) and has therefore singehandedly discovered a "cure" for the virus.

I, too, believe it was a blessing from God, but I need another week or two to find out if I was correct.

Oct 7, 2020 9:11 PM

Special thanks to the fly that landed on Mike Pence during tonight's debate.

Mother doesn't like anybody messing with Mike's fly.

Oct 9, 2020 4:16 PM

Ladies and germs, your president*, today on Fox: "If you fuck around with us, if you do something bad to us, we are gonna do things to you that have never been done before."

He's lost all control of himself. Soon he'll be eating a soft diet and wondering what's the combination to the keypad that keeps the door locked.

Oct 10, 2020 7:10 AM

Gilligan's Titanic: Isn't it fine to wake up and know for certain you are far richer than Trump?

As long as you owe less than $400 million, you're much better off! My God! I think I'll order that solid-gold toilet after all.

Oct 10, 2020 8:43 AM
Imagine broadcasters in ancient Rome trying to decide whether to discuss Caligula's mental condition on the air.

Oct 10, 2020 3:56 PM
Did you know that Hunter Biden used to be chairman of the board of the World Food Program USA, the mother organization of which won the Nobel Prize this week for fighting hunger in trouble spots all over the world?
That's what he was doing while Cokehead Junior and Fredo Trump were killing endangered species in Africa, for fun.

Oct 10, 2020 5:54 PM
Dan Quayle has endorsed Donald Trumpe.

Oct 12, 2020 8:56 AM
Amy Coney Barrett disqualifies herself because she let herself be nominated by this person, in this way, at this time. This is what proves she does not have the judgment to sit on the Supreme Court.

Oct 12, 2020 7:33 PM
Trump threw virus-tainted masks to his fans at the Florida rally, commemorating the smallpox-laden blankets presented to Natives by the Pilgrims at the first Thanksgiving.

Oct 12, 2020 9:22 PM
Crawling with antibodies, livid with a steroid flush and bluster, flying on massive infusions of fetal stem cells + all the performance enhancers in Dr. Twinkly's Magic Bag, Trump spreads an infectious message of victory over disease through personal exposure to his own germs.

Oct 14, 2020 3:21 PM
Is Covid-19 the first thing Trump ever gave Barron?

Oct 15, 2020 9:14 PM

Biden showed up at his town hall and answered every question calmly.

Trump ranted, raved, sweated, raged, and grinned like a fish when the lady from "Ancient Aliens" told him his beautiful smile made him so handsome.

The Republicans are complaining that Joe is "so boring." They like American life as an extended Jerry Springer episode. The rest of us are so ready to shut down this horrible unreality show.

Let's just take a moment to savor the fact that Trump lost a debate at which he was the only candidate in attendance.

Oct 16, 2020 4:12 PM

Thinking about Melania coming into the White House thinking she would be the most glamorous, photographed, fabulous Jackie O celebrity in the world, and now she's the fast-aging moll of a failed politician, shoved into a corner, with a hacking cough that won't go away.

Oct 17, 2020 3:44 PM

JFK Jr. came over this afternoon. We had some brews and watched the first part of the Bama game. We watched a few minutes of Trump saying Melania told him he was better looking than JFK Sr. We had a pretty good laff at that one. JFK Jr. calls Trump "Booboo" and does this great Yogi Bear imitation of him. I invited him to stay for dinner but he had to fly. "Q gonna Q," as he put it. I said I hoped he didn't mean that literally and he said "you know I do all my flying on the turnpike these days." He drives a Hyundai, who'da thunk.

Oct 18, 2020 10:53 AM

Maybe it's good politics to gather thousands of your supporters, unmasked, in the states with the hottest Covid hot spots.

Or maybe it's the politics of a madman, with a substantial portion of the population following him into madness.

Never seen rallies where people would risk their own and others' lives in order to scream their approval at the worst person in the world. Well, not in the last 80 years or so, anyway. Even Hitler's fanatics didn't go to Nuremberg to deliberately infect each other as a political statement.

Oct 18, 2020 7:59 PM
Trump says Biden is going to "cancel Christmas." That should convince Melania to vote for Biden since we now know how much she hates "that fucking Christmas stuff."

Oct 19, 2020 10:51 AM
Qanon is a Russian disinformation project currently sponsored by the Republican Party.

Oct 20, 2020 5:24 PM
Melania bailed out of traveling to Pennsylvania tonight because she reported a "lingering cough" and a "huge pain in the ass."

Oct 20, 2020 7:45 PM
Presidential* Rage Report: Trump began the day in a Simmering Rage, blew into a Towering Rage shortly after midday, spent the afternoon in a Furious Rage, pivoted to a Violent Rage for the dinner hour and wound up the evening in a Blind Bitter Rage. Morning forecast: Impotent Rage.

Oct 21, 2020 8:54 AM
Trumpy is an innovative campaigner. Last night he flew to Erie, Pennsylvania to tell the people at his superspreader rally that 1/ he didn't want to be in Erie, 2/ it's ridiculous the race is so close he had to go to Erie, 3/ it was too chilly, 4/ he will never come back if he wins, and in closing, 5/ you are losers and suckers and I wish I was anywhere else. Please like me! Goodbye!

Oct 21, 2020 11:33 AM

I knew something was going to make me happy today, but I did not have "Rudy Giuliani stung by Borat" on my list!

Oct 24, 2020 3:34 PM

The last time somebody spanked Trump as hard as Obama just did in that campaign speech, Trump had to pay her $130,000 to keep quiet about it.

Oct 25, 2020 8:52 PM

I'll just point out that the question that led Trump to flee "60 Minutes'" Lesley Stahl, quaking with rage, was "are you ready for some tough questions?"

Oct 26, 2020 11:12 AM

Late Stage GOP Campaign Tactics, Advanced: The day after your Chief of Staff announces you've surrendered to the virus, send your universally despised trust-baby son-in-law out to lecture Black people about their lack of ambition.

Oct 27, 2020 8:14 AM

He walked Amy Coney Barrett up on our balcony like Evita and stood her there to be admired as his political prize.

She smiled and waved and accepted the cheers of the super-spreading crowd.

Coney is forever Trump's justice. She is stained for every day of her lifetime appointment. She might have said "let's wait on this vote until after the election," and both sides would have hailed her judicial temperament. Instead she chose the path of Trump.

Everything Trump touches turns to shit. She'll find out.

Oct 28, 2020 7:06 AM

While you were sleeping, the Trump campaign abandoned hundreds of his rallygoers after last night's rally at an Omaha airport.

The buses that had taken them from their cars to the rally site failed to appear after the rally ended. Thousands, including many elderly people, were forced to walk between three and seven miles to their cars. Dozens were treated for hypothermia and exhaustion. Police gave rides to quite a few. No telling how many were infected by Covid-19, but of course they'd all signed up for the superspreader rally.

Luckily:
1. Trump flew away in Air Force One, so his toes never got cold
2. The buses will be there in two weeks
3. The buses, when they arrive, will be the most beautiful and plentiful buses, the warmest and most comfortable buses anyone has ever seen
4. Hunter Biden cancelled the buses to buy coke
5. Brad Parscale spent all the bus money on a new Ferrari, and intended to come give some people rides, but realized that he could only take one passenger at a time, so he stayed home to continue beating his wife
6. If you are still walking along a freezing Nebraska road, don't worry. You are rounding the bend!
7. This incident was rejected by the Department of Metaphor for being too "on the nose"

Oct 29, 2020 10:22 PM
I sent a check to my bank via USPS, but someone stole the package and sliced it open and took the check out, and changed the name on the "pay" line" to "Donald J. Trump," and sent the check to Trump, who cashed it, and bought some solid gold toilet paper, but then Hunter Biden came in and stole my baby, and sold the baby for drugs, he sold it to Hillary who ate the baby in her secret basement pizza parlor. Some of this is speculation, but most of it is just common sense. Don't Mask Me!

Oct 30, 2020 3:30 PM
Let's take a moment to step back and breathe. And observe what is happening in front of our eyes.

A pandemic rages. Trump is planning a series of 17 superspreader rallies between now and Monday night, flying around on your airplane at your expense to states where the virus is spiking to record levels every single day.

This is the elected leader of the country spreading and inflaming pockets of disease during a pandemic, when most of the country is still hiding and wearing masks and staying away from loved ones. His 17 rallies will increase levels of infection in 17 cities. Does anybody think this is winning him votes?

A traveling show of disease! A virus victory dance! A mass orgy of mask-free celebrants dancing to "YMCA" and telling this virus to go fuck itself, as they spray each other with droplets!

This spectacle is nothing we have ever seen or will ever see again. Observe, friends, the vivid and literal disintegration of the American psyche. This country has officially lost its damn mind.

Oct 31, 2020 6:14 PM

Right now Bourbon Street is full of out-of-town partiers who are refusing to wear a mask ... on HALLOWEEN!

Nov 1, 2020 12:55 PM

Everybody is writing to me now, so urgently, 10 or 12 emails an hour. Barack swears, "this is the last time I'll ask." Kamala writes, "Mark, this is urgent!' Joe Biden says "last time I'll ask," but he said that yesterday! And the day before that! Even Doug Emhoff is writing to me, as if maybe I'll listen to him especially, perhaps the others might forget to ask me again - "Hey Mark I know we're asking a lot but...."

To all of these my dear candidate pals I say, "Hey, algorithm, you really ought to come up with an automated message that kicks in along the lines of....

"Hey Mark, this is Barack and Joe, this is your ole pal Elizabeth, this is your rejected lover Pete, we know we have asked and asked and asked, and damned if you didn't shower us with more cash than has ever been given by small OR large donors in any campaign in history, like $350 million just last month, like more than a billion overall, like

DOUBLE what the Republicans gave to Trump - and we have enough now, we can do these last two days on what you already gave us. So just RELAX and CHILL and WE GOT THIS thank you good night!"

Nov 2, 2020 10:35 AM
From the very first moment you realized the Covid-19 pandemic was coming to America, didn't you always know that one day it would come down to Trump blaming the doctors?

Nov 3, 2020 6:48 AM

D: Everybody says I'm going to lose
M: Is true
D: They all seem pretty happy about it, too
M: Will be big party
D: They said that in 2016 too
M: Now they hating you more
D: Who are you calling?
M: Justin
D: Trudeau?
M: Else who?

Nov 3, 2020 7:28 AM
Trump got up this morning, sipped a cup of Celestial Seasonings tea, and took a long meditative stroll in the Rose Garden with Melania. They talked about funny little moments they'd shared in the White House, their dreams of a retirement home after the next term is over. Sleepy Barron loped out onto the lawn to toss the ball with Dad in the early morning light. For this brief moment, the three of them were truly happy, and they knew the second term would be even better.

Nov 3, 2020 8:51 AM
At his final rally in Michigan, Trump insulted LeBron James, Lady Gaga, and Jon Bon Jovi, and complained that Fox News gave him much more help in the 2016 campaign.

"I had a very easy life before this," Trump said.

O Malodorous Fool! We all had a very easy life before you! And today we will take that life back!

Nov 3, 2020 10:14 AM

One way or the other, I'm having a party tonight.

Nov 4, 2020 1:40 AM

I still think Joe Biden won and will win. But I think the phrase "this is not who we are" can now safely be retired. This is who many of us are.

Nov 5, 2020 9:34 AM

Watching these vote counts dragging on is like waiting for Christmas morning if you aren't sure whether Santa Claus is going to bring you presents or hack you to death with a machete.

Nov 5, 2020 6:33 PM

The losing loser is badly losing, proving how not to lose, showing that losing is what losers do, strongly and powerfully losing. The losiest loser ever. Losing most lositively. When you're a star they let you lose, they don't even ask, you just lose.

Nov 6, 2020 9:45 PM

D: This is all your fault. That stupid coat with the writing on the back
M: Oh please. Off you fuck
D: Things went downhill when I married you
M: I was #1 Slovenia girl so much happy
D: Your double is nicer than you, younger too
M: Sleep with him then, if you like him so much

Donald J. Trump ✔ @realDonaldTrump · 1h
We have claimed, for Electoral Vote purposes, the Commonwealth of Pennsylvania (which won't allow legal observers) the State of Georgia, and the State of North Carolina, each one of which has a BIG Trump lead. Additionally, we hereby claim the State of Michigan if, in fact,.....

(!) Official sources may not have called the race when this was Tweeted

💬 89.8K   🔁 89.3K   ♡ 183.4K   ⬆

Abraham Lincoln
@SurrealALincoln

Replying to @realDonaldTrump

I Abraham, son of Robert, hereby claim all Lands west of the Mississippi, all sweet gals named Mary, all faithful dogs and skeptical house cats, every biscuit ever baked, stovepipe hats in every shade of black, oh and also the State of Michigan! if, in fact,.....

5:14 PM · Nov 4, 2020 · Twitter Web App

Nov 7, 2020 7:04 AM

T: You! What are you doing here?
　　(A dark figure steps forward, face shadowed)
H: You know why I'm here
T: No! I won't! I won't conceive!
H: It's "concede," Donald. This is the Talk. It's over. You're through.

T: Nooo! Why is it YOU? How did you get in here?

Hillary: This used to be my bathroom. I still have a key. And I'm the only who ever tells you the truth to your face.

Nov 7, 2020 9:41 AM

Only in America with its Slaveholder College could the man who is leading by four million votes still be fighting to win the election.

Nov 7, 2020 10:26 AM

CNN and NBC call it. Biden is elected. Hallelujah!

Nov 7, 2020 11:14 AM

Dancing in the streets

Nov 7, 2020 5:04 PM

The gracious concession we all knew was coming:

Donald J. Trump ✓
@realDonaldTrump

THE OBSERVERS WERE NOT ALLOWED INTO THE COUNTING ROOMS. I WON THE ELECTION, GOT 71,000,000 LEGAL VOTES. BAD THINGS HAPPENED WHICH OUR OBSERVERS WERE NOT ALLOWED TO SEE. NEVER HAPPENED BEFORE. MILLIONS OF MAIL-IN BALLOTS WERE SENT TO PEOPLE WHO NEVER ASKED FOR THEM!

① This claim about election fraud is disputed

3:53 PM · Nov 7, 2020   ⓘ

♡ 678K   ♡ 413.2K people are Tweeting about this

Nov 7, 2020 6:34 PM

I'm thinking the Trump Presidential Library can just be an app.

Nov 7, 2020 10:15 PM

Meet me at Four Seasons.
Hotel?
No, landscaping
Where?
Next to the dildo shop
Which one?
Across from the crematorium

THE END

AUTHOR'S NOTE

Many of the entries in my journal have appeared in some form on Facebook, Twitter, and other sites, for an audience of staunch resisters that grew in number as the surreality of Trump's rise became clear. Other portions appeared in different forms in the Wall Street Journal and other publications. Although I have selected and edited the entries, I have tried to preserve every one of my most embarrassing prognostications for the reader to enjoy. Thanks to all those who believed that we could summon the collective will to vote him out. Stay tuned...

– MGC

ABOUT THE AUTHOR

Mark Childress, a native of Monroeville, Alabama, is a novelist, journalist, and screenwriter. His seven novels have been published in eleven languages, and his essays and stories have appeared in the New York Times, Los Angeles Times, Wall Street Journal,and many other publications. He has lived in the USA, Spain, Costa Rica, and Viet Nam. Currently makes his home on the planet New Orleans.